IA DORE is Head of Midwifery and **ROS BRADBURY** ...oordinator Midwife at the Princess Anne Hospital, Scuthampton. Both appeared in the first two series of Channel 4's Bafta-winning *One Born Every Minute*.

ONE BORN EVERY MINUTE

REAL STORIES FROM THE DELIVERY ROOM

MARIA DORE AND ROS BRADBURY

as told to

DIANE TAYLOR

SPHERE

First published in Great Britain in 2011 by Sphere
This revised edition first published in 2012
Reprinted 2012

A CIP catalogue record for this book
is available from the British Library.

ISBN 978-0-7515-4600-2

Typeset in Bembo by M Rules
Printed and bound in Great Britain by
Clays Ltd, St Ives plc

Papers used by Sphere are from well-managed forests
and other responsible sources.

MIX
Paper from
responsible sources
FSC® C104740

Sphere
An imprint of
Little, Brown Book Group
100 Victoria Embankment
London EC4Y 0DY

An Hachette UK Company
www.hachette.co.uk

www.littlebrown.co.uk

CONTENTS

The babies born at the Princess Anne Hospital in Southampton, during the first two series of *One Born Every Minute*, were welcomed not only by proud mums and dads and anxious friends and families, but by millions of viewers who were glued to their television screens at home.

Over twenty episodes, we have been allowed unique and privileged access to incredibly intimate and emotional moments, and we also got to know a supporting cast of quiet heroes: the staff at the Princess Anne Hospital. We watched them calmly guiding countless women through labour, but also caught glimpses of them off-duty: relaxing over a much-needed cuppa and a slice of homemade cake; sharing a joke and a gossip; celebrating with colleagues and, most of all, still amazed by the births they witness every day.

Midwives Maria and Ros have many wonderful stories from throughout their careers, and here they share their memories – also drawing on the experiences of their colleagues – to shed light on what life is *really* like for a modern midwife.

1

WHO WANTS TO BE A MIDWIFE?

You never quite get over that miracle
Maria, episode 8

ROS

I was born and grew up in Scotland, the middle child of five. From a very early age I was a tomboy, far more interested in climbing trees than playing with dolls. When I wasn't playing outside, I would read all the time – I read before breakfast, I read while I was walking to school and I read by the light of street lamps. I devoured all the books I could get my hands on, and was particularly keen on school stories, like Elinor Brent-Dyer's Chalet School series. I longed to be sent away to boarding school like the girls in these books. It sounded like much more fun than living at home with my family! My parents weren't too keen to oblige me on that particular whim, however, and like my brothers and sisters, I attended the local school.

As a child I was always intrigued by hospitals and was amazed at the way they could make poorly people better. It seemed like magic to me, and I wasn't at all unhappy when I had to go into hospital, aged twelve, to have something removed from the sole of my foot. While I was there I became friendly with some of the other young patients, and one day a nurse came into the room to find a group of us sitting on one of the beds, crying. She asked us what was wrong, and everyone else wailed that they wanted to go home, but had been told they must stay in for a bit longer. Not me. I was crying because I'd been told I had to go home! I loved the atmosphere in the hospital so much that I would have been happy to have stayed there for ever. To me it seemed just like the boarding schools I loved to read about, with everyone away from home together, having fun and sleeping in the same room. I loved the clean, hospital smell, the way they could fix the broken bits of people. There was also something about the order and efficiency of hospital life that appealed to me.

But despite this fascination with all things medical, when I was a little girl I really wanted to be a librarian. I'd dream about reading all day long, interrupted only by the occasional borrower asking for their book to be stamped. By the time I was a teenager though, I'd had a change of heart and decided that I wanted to study medicine and become a doctor. I'm sure that in some small way, my happy memories of the hospital when I was younger played a part in this decision. I had always enjoyed maths and chemistry – to this day I still love numbers and whenever I have a spare moment I take out my Sudoku puzzles. So, medicine seemed like an obvious choice, although I also loved English, which wasn't such a useful subject for a future doctor.

I wasn't happy at school and was desperate to leave. I felt a bit of a misfit – I got on well with the other pupils, but I didn't have any really close friends and I was keen to move onto the next stage. Although I have a good brain, I must admit that I didn't work as hard as I could have done and didn't quite get the grades I needed to study medicine, so I went onto a waiting list. I had also applied to do a nursing degree as a safety net, and I was offered a place on that course straight away. I should have been thrilled, but they needed me to make my mind up pretty quickly and I wasn't sure what to do. What about the career in medicine I'd set my heart on? Could I be happy as a nurse, taking orders from doctors? It was a difficult decision that I mulled over for some time, but in the end I realised that if I turned this place down and didn't get a place at medical school, I'd be left with nothing. I chose what seemed like the safest option and embarked on a nursing degree.

I did find the course a real struggle at first – it took me a while to reconcile myself to studying nursing rather than medicine. I would see lots of medical students milling around, and longed to be with them. I was convinced that

I'd made the wrong decision to study nursing, but decided that now I'd started I better just carry on and make the best of it. Thankfully, the more I did of the course the more I enjoyed it. You can spend a lot of time saying, 'What if . . .' or, 'I wish I'd done that differently', but when I look at the way my life has turned out, I have absolutely no regrets.

As I said, I'm not the most dedicated student and can be lazy about studying – I wrote all my essays the night before they were due in! But work aside, I had a great time at university and a lively social life. As time went by, I thought less and less about what would have been if I'd trained as a doctor. I enjoyed nursing and looked forward to the time when I'd be based full-time in a hospital, helping to make people better.

It's true what they say about the grass always being greener on the other side of the fence. I have friends who are doctors and get to hear all the pros and cons from them. Medicine certainly is a good career, but like everything else it has its downside. My female doctor colleagues have to make big choices and sacrifices if they want to have a family – either they have to work full-time and miss out on their children, or work part-time and delay advancing their career.

I enjoyed a lot of the placements I did as a student. I spent six months working on a neuro-surgical ward which was very demanding and hi-tech and four weeks with a district nurse, treating patients in the surgery and doing home visits.

4

I saw a huge variety of conditions and met some really interesting people. But most of all, I loved the four weeks I spent as an observer in the midwifery unit. My month-long maternity stint was at Simpsons Maternity Unit at the Royal Infirmary in Edinburgh. All we were expected to do at that point was observe others delivering babies – they didn't let us novices anywhere near the real action! To be honest, I don't remember being bowled over by the miracle of life when I saw a baby being born for the first time. My mum was a midwife before she had children of her own, so perhaps because of her, I was never particularly curious about the mechanics of pregnancy and birth – it didn't seem like some great mystery to me. I'm not conscious of my mum being an influence on my eventual career choice, but perhaps subliminally she was. I do remember that I thought midwifery would be a useful qualification to have and so I applied to do an eighteen-month course in Southampton when I'd completed my degree.

One way or another there's quite a lot of medical training in my family. As I said, mum had worked as a midwife when she was young, and later on she trained as a teacher, taught for quite a few years and then worked on a Medical Research Council project attached to a general practice. My brother became a paediatrician and one of my sisters also became a nurse. Of my two younger sisters one is a teacher and the other did a law degree, but now she and her husband are missionaries.

In Edinburgh I had shared a flat with an English Literature student who married a medical student in Southampton. She was the one who persuaded me to move away from Edinburgh.

'Why not come down to Southampton?' she said. 'It's lovely down here. There's a brand new maternity hospital and it's by the sea!'

So that's what I did. At university I had never been homesick because my family were living just twenty miles away. But when I arrived in Southampton to begin midwifery, it was the furthest away from home I'd ever been and I was really homesick. My younger sister was about to have a baby and I felt I was too far away from my family. Again, I wondered if I'd made a mistake.

Although I was miserable at first, I did gradually adjust to living in a new place. The course was busy and very varied and we did three-month stints in different areas of midwifery. I spent time working with a community midwife and a district nurse, as well as on the wards. Going into different people's houses was quite an eye opener, and it was fascinating to see how people live in so many different ways. Some places I visited I didn't want to sit down on the chairs because they were so dirty, but as a midwife you have a duty of care to the woman in that house, and you have to get on with it and do whatever needs to be done. It's important to remember that you're a guest in the women's home — they don't have to let you in and it's important to show them respect.

The part of my training that I enjoyed most was the time I spent on labour ward. I loved the buzz and excitement of the place, and I felt at home in the hospital environment. Most of our clients are fit, healthy women who leave hospital with a beautiful baby. It's nice to look after mostly well women who are doing something that is very natural. It's hard to imagine a more satisfying job than helping bring new life into the world and seeing families go home over-joyed with the new addition to their family.

After I'd completed my midwifery training I had to decide where I wanted to work. I knew that I didn't want to go home to Edinburgh, because I felt that the births there were handled in a more doctor-focused way. I also knew that in other parts of the country midwives had more autonomy and I was keen to be able to work in that way.

One of the things that really appealed to me about mid-wifery is the level of responsibility you have compared with a lot of other areas of nursing. I think I've been very fortunate in my career, because over the years the role of the midwife has expanded – we're capable of giving more holistic care to women. As a midwife you can be an autonomous practitioner and unless there are complications, doctors don't need to be involved. It's up to me to assess the situation, to plan a course of action and to make decisions: the buck stops with me.

I met Simon, the man who was to become my husband, in Southampton. He was a cadet in the merchant navy and was originally from Birmingham. We decided to get married, but he didn't want to live in Scotland and I didn't want to live in Birmingham so we compromised and decided to stay in Southampton. I've been here for twenty-eight years now, and aside from those first few months of homesickness, I've never regretted it.

Simon left the navy and did a series of jobs before joining the police force. It's funny, quite a few of the midwives are married to policemen. I suppose it's because both are people-centred jobs, both have a '999' element to them and both involve shift work. It's much easier to cope with the demands of a job like ours when you know that your partner understands exactly what you're going through. We have four children, the oldest is in her twenties and the youngest is still a teenager. I had always wanted four – with my love of order and numbers I liked the idea of having an even number of children, and feel very blessed to have such a wonderful and loving family.

Simon and I both worked when the children were small, which was sometimes difficult. Although he is a fantastic dad, there were certain things that the children only wanted mum for when they were small, but I wasn't able to drop everything and run home to dole out cuddles and kiss sore knees better when I was about to deliver a baby. We have always managed to organise our shifts so that we could share out the childcare and we just about managed it between us. I often couldn't stay behind at the end of a night shift, even if a woman I'd looked after all night was likely to give birth in the next half an hour or so, because I had to rush home to relieve Simon and get the kids to school. Doing the jobs we do, we have learned not to expect each other through the door at a certain time. Luckily our children have always been very understanding – I suppose it's what they've always known. We do our best to be there for special events in their lives, but can't always get to sports days and school concerts because we're working or sleeping. I think that our way of working has taught them how to be flexible.

It's hard for a midwife to be spontaneous about aspects of life outside of work, because shifts are worked out well in advance. It's not such a problem to request a shift swap for an event a few months away, like a wedding, but trickier to change your duty for an event a few days away, unless you can find another midwife to switch shifts with you.

As with other parts of the medical profession and emergency services, we offer a round-the-clock service. We have to take our turn to work Christmas and New Year, which is very hard from the children's point of view. There were many years when I worked Christmas Eve night – I would leave Simon in charge of filling the children's stockings and appear home in time for Christmas morning. I'd be able to muster enough energy to make it through the presents, but by the afternoon I'd be getting drowsy and would soon be fast asleep. The children begged me to work a different shift, but if I worked on Christmas night, the thought of having to leave the family at the end of Christmas Day cast a bit of a pall over the proceedings. There is just no easy way to combine midwifery and family life at Christmastime.

When I worked nights after I first qualified I really struggled to stay awake and then do the twenty-minute drive home. And although I was exhausted, I found it hard to sleep properly during the day. But not any more. As soon as I get home from my night shift, I crawl into bed and I'm out like a light and usually get about six hours of sleep, which is more than some of my colleagues manage.

I enjoy working nights because there are fewer staff on duty and often there's more of a team spirit – it's just the midwives, three obstetricians and one anaesthetist on duty. And there's a consultant on call at home for dire emergencies. There really is something special about night duty. Because there are fewer people around, you can build up a real affinity with the woman you're looking after. By the time the baby has been delivered there's a special camaraderie; a sense of having survived the whole experience together.

During the night women who are in the early stages of labour and those who have had epidurals are encouraged to sleep. The more rest the woman can get, the better prepared she'll be for giving birth. The downside is that if it's just the midwife, the slumbering woman, her partner dozing in the chair and the monitor bleeping in a dimly lit room, it can be very hard for us midwives to stay awake. But the more night duty I've done, the more my body has adjusted to the demands of this work and I've learnt a few tricks of the trade along the way, such as snacking – usually on something healthy like carrot sticks – to stave off the tiredness.

While this is a wonderful job, it is easy to see it through rose-coloured spectacles as a student – it can appear to be all bouncing babies and joyful mothers. The daily reality is a little different! As a midwife it doesn't matter how *you* feel – you have to be professional and you have to take the good with the bad. Sometimes things can go wrong; horrible tragedies not only for the mother and her family, but also for us. But even in desperate situations, it's important to remain professional, not to run away even if that's sometimes what you feel like doing and to offer extra support to the woman and her family.

We're used to seeing women behave irrationally because they're under so much stress. We accept that labour is an exceptional and highly emotional experience, and that women often don't behave the way they would the rest of the time. Often a woman arrives in the labour ward and appears to be very polite and well-mannered, but as her labour progresses she might start to come out with incredibly bad language. We try not to stereotype people, but I'm still sometimes surprised when the air turns particularly blue and think to myself, 'I never imagined this woman would use *that* kind of language!'

Of course, sometimes it works the other way, too. There are times when I know a woman can push her baby out, but she's not pushing properly. She needs to pull herself together and really focus on pushing. On those occasions I go into 'firm' mode and say, 'This has to stop. Next time you have a contraction, don't waste all your effort screaming. You can't push with your throat.' I remember once, when I'd had to be quite firm, the new mum turned to me and said, accusingly, 'You were mean to me!'

'But you pushed the baby out, didn't you? I wasn't being mean, I was just telling you what you needed to do to get your baby out,' I replied.

Midwives are usually sympathetic and kind, and it can be quite difficult to suddenly change gear and say, 'Stop this nonsense and follow my instructions next time you push.' That's when it can be quite useful for a senior midwife like me to come in, in the final stages, to support the woman and the midwife, both of whom may be flagging. I'm quite happy to be the tough one who tells the woman she has to push – the bad cop to the other midwife's good cop – if it helps get the baby out.

Working as a midwife at Princess Anne Hospital is like having a second family. It's a very friendly place, everyone says hello to each other and you get to know a lot about the lives of other staff.

Most of the midwives are women but we do have two

male midwives – in fact, one of them is married to another midwife. But a lot of the time it's just women staffing the labour ward. And it seems like at any one time there's always at least one midwife who's pregnant! Sometimes the pregnant midwife chooses a friend or a senior midwife to look after them during the pregnancy, although often they're happy to be looked after by whoever is on duty.

I've delivered babies for quite a few of my friends and I have found it a real privilege. There are some midwives who would rather not look after friends because there's a personal relationship and so they might worry if things went wrong. Some people just find it a bit awkward. When you look after someone you know, you already have a mutual understanding and trust and know their husband or partner as well. It certainly makes for a different atmosphere in the delivery room. Some midwives I know have looked after their own daughters in labour – I'm not sure how I would feel about doing that for one of my daughters. I think that relationship is too close, and it might be hard to separate professional and maternal feelings.

One friend whose baby I delivered was singing during the contractions and wanted us all to sing along with her. We were singing, 'What Shall We Do With the Drunken Sailor'. She changed the words to something unrepeatable, and it was absolutely hilarious. Birth can be a very painful business but there's also plenty of scope to have a good giggle.

One friend I looked after had her baby while I was pregnant with my fourth child. She was having her first and had tried everything to kick-start labour. In the end, she had to be induced and ended up having a Caesarean section – it was a long haul and including the induction the whole thing took about three days. A few months later I gave birth to my fourth child. I went into labour in the night and delivered her a few hours later early in the morning. I was due to meet this friend for coffee that morning, and had to call her to say I wouldn't be able to make it because I'd just given birth ... I'm not sure I was her favourite person at that point!

While there are some universal truths about labour and childbirth, it's impossible to generalise. Every woman is unique and every woman's experience of labour is unique. For some women it's hugely reassuring to be looked after by a friend, while others prefer to be looked after by an anonymous stranger that they never need to see again.

A lot of people like the 'cuddling the babies' side of childbirth, but not so much the messy parts. People ask me, 'How can you do a job like that with all the mess and the blood?' I just laugh and say that when it comes to childbirth, a whole variety of bodily fluids are part of the package.

Childbirth really is a time when just about every fluid manufactured by the human body puts in an appearance – sometimes all at the same time! The baby and placenta are bloodied and the 'waters' – the membrane surrounding the baby – is a bodily fluid unique to childbirth. Women sometimes vomit, urinate or lose control of their bowels during labour. You definitely need to have a cast-iron constitution, to be a midwife and if you don't have that when you start the job it certainly develops over time!

When I was a student nurse I used to faint quite a lot because I have low blood pressure. But I learnt to keep myself moving and make sure that I was drinking enough to keep my fluid levels up. You just learn to deal with whatever presents itself to you.

Some women see me as a human being, rather than just someone in a uniform who takes their blood pressure and delivers the baby. I don't push information about myself on them, but I always respond when they ask me questions about myself. Often having a nice friendly chat with a woman is the best way to offer advice about feeding, the things that might be causing the baby to cry, advice about how warmly to dress the baby and how soon after birth to start exercising.

There are some women who I've grown quite close to during their labour and have really connected with them. Sometimes I look after a woman and think, this is the sort of person I'd be friendly with outside work. I looked after a woman a couple of years ago who was having a termination because there were severe abnormalities in the foetus.

The whole thing was very sad, but during the process we talked about everything. At a time when I would have expected her to be withdrawn and introspective, she managed to retain her sense of humour. Afterwards she sent me a card to thank me for looking after her. I was very touched when she said that I'd made a very difficult experience a little bit easier for her.

MARIA

When I was growing up, I never dreamed about having a career as a midwife. In fact, I never dreamed of having any particular career at all! I started going out with my husband when I was fifteen and it was a relationship that flourished. I had no ambitions to do anything other than be happy, and falling in love just came naturally. I was one of those children at school whose report card always said, 'Maria is capable of much more if only she would focus', but my focus was always on having fun and enjoying life.

So I left school with two A-levels and had no intentions of going to university. I wanted to get a job, earn some money and get married. In a very short space of time I had a succession of short-term jobs, working at Marks & Spencer's in the men's department, and then on a production line for contact lenses. Both of which taught me I was not cut out for tidying shelves or detailed repetitive work.

Then I branched out into life insurance, where I managed to persuade people to invest in policies I didn't really understand – including a butcher and a funeral director. I realised that I didn't want to sell anything I didn't believe in, and so escaped into a job at the National Westminster Bank in Eastleigh. I started at the bottom, counting cheques, and every day my goal was to find another job as soon as possible. Finance was not for me!

I spotted an advert for student nurse placements at Winchester and decided to apply. This decision wasn't triggered by a Florence Nightingale-type calling – to be honest, what really appealed to me was leaving home and having a room of my own! My family were astonished by this sudden decision because I had always hated needles, knives and the sight of blood. They reckoned that the only thing that would stand me in good stead was that I was good at talking. Turns out they weren't wrong. I was interviewed by a delightful tutor; a kind man with an enormous beard. Somehow, all the right things seemed to roll off my tongue. I told him that I thought I'd make a fantastic nurse and would always put the patient first. I must have convinced him, because I was offered a place on the course.

From the word go, I absolutely loved nursing. I enjoyed working with so many different people and interacting with such a varied cross-section of society. I felt a very strong empathy with the patients I looked after, and used to get very upset when dealing with terminal cases. I remember nursing a gentle Russian man who had been diagnosed with stomach cancer. Although I was an ex-convent girl I wasn't a practising Catholic, but I was so upset by his diagnosis that I went into the chapel to say a prayer for him. I don't know what happened to him as I didn't stay on that ward, but his prognosis was not good and I found that incredibly hard to deal with.

It was a whole year into my training before I plucked up the courage to give an injection. I was fine when we practised injecting oranges, but the thought of injecting a real person absolutely turned my stomach. I didn't know how I was going to overcome this phobia, but I realised that if I wanted to be a nurse I couldn't go on avoiding giving injections. So one day, I took a deep breath, plunged the needle into an unsuspecting patient and discovered that it wasn't quite as bad as I'd thought it was. And the patient survived too! As I got more and more used to giving injections, my phobia subsided and I actually became quite good at it – or so my patients said.

When I was twenty I got married to my husband, then and now the love of my life. Soon after that, I qualified, became a staff nurse and started wondering what I should do next. I was working as a staff nurse on a mixed-sex medical ward and really enjoyed the moments when a quick response to an emergency such as a cardiac arrest was required. The rush of adrenaline as you worked as a team to save a life and the subsequent reward when with good nursing care the patient would go home. Therefore I knew that whatever my next job was, it would need to allow for variation in routine, high level of expertise in nursing care and the potential for happy results.

During my training I had really enjoyed the children's ward and although I hadn't liked my maternity placement I knew that as a staff nurse I could have the opportunity to do further training in either of those areas and so decided to choose something slightly in the middle to help me make up my mind – I applied for a job in a baby neo-natal unit at Southampton. There I found myself looking after between one and three incredibly small babies – they seemed to me just like little fledglings. My cases included anything from a baby born at twenty-four weeks to a full-term poorly baby. The twenty-four-weekers looked like tiny, bony birds straight out of the nest. This was quite a contrast to my previous nursing experience. Working in the neo-natal unit was very emotional. We would celebrate a poorly baby's tiny step forward, but then that baby might take a few steps back. In these circumstances it's very important to nurture the parents as well as the baby. It can be quite a challenge to keep the parents upbeat.

One of my jobs on the neo-natal unit was to go onto the labour ward to receive the babies. In those days the neo-natal nurse would accompany the paediatrician for a '2' or '3' bell call to labour ward. '2' bells were for forceps or ventouse deliveries that were planned, and '3' bells meant it was more urgent and there were concerns about the baby's safety. We would also wait in theatre for babies born by emergency Caesarean sections. Our role was to receive the baby as it was born and to assist the paediatrician with any resuscitation of the baby that was required.

I absolutely loved the atmosphere and the buzz of the labour ward and decided that this was the route I wanted my career to take. I applied to do the eighteen-month course at Southampton and was accepted to do my midwifery training. I think I was really fortunate because the midwives on labour ward already knew me and took me under their wings as I became a student for the second time. One of the Senior Sisters, Mary Nolan, was my mentor on labour ward – a gently spoken Irish woman with a slightly austere appearance. Although I hardly ever had the opportunity to work with her because she was always in charge, I felt she always put me with a midwife who was a confident teacher and enjoyed working with students, so my experience was really rewarding.

The pace of work in midwifery is very different to nursing. Nursing can be very process driven, whereas midwifery is very much a partnership with the mother. I believe care in midwifery tends to be more considered, because it is often planned and discussed with the mother in advance and the role of the midwife is often one of educator. Women are usually healthy and want to be involved. It's a lesson you learn early in your training.

Novices often learn by their mistakes and have to hope that these mistakes aren't too terrible. I can remember, very early on, wrapping up a baby following a birth and placing it on the resuscitaire whilst I went and washed my hands – I just walked over to the other side of the room, not thinking twice about it. One of the senior sisters sidled up to me and whispered in my ear, 'Do you really think you should leave that baby unattended on the resuscitaire?'

I was mortified, clapping my hand over my mouth in horror as I realised what I had done. Later in my career I have laughed with Marlene Newman, the sister who pointed out my thoughtless act, at the way we were introduced. Marlene was the midwife who delivered both my children and also helped me with my study for my midwifery finals. She will still hold me to account if she thinks I could do something better.

I soon grew to love the job. That moment of anticipation, just before the baby comes out, is one of the most magical things in the world. Everyone's holding their breath, willing it all to work out fine and when the baby does emerge, there's this absolute explosion of joy and relief. It's an incredibly emotional moment and there's nothing else like it in life. I felt totally elated to be sharing in this special moment that most people aren't privy to. Although I've delivered many babies over the years, that feeling never diminishes. Birth is just such an amazing event.

★

I always wanted to be a young mum and so chose to have my son and daughter quite early in my career. My daughter, Rebecca, was my first born. I had a miserable pregnancy with her – my first few months were filled with nausea and then my hands and feet became really puffy. I had a friend who said that 'through great pain and suffering comes great beauty'. I think she may have been right. I took the statutory maternity leave and returned to work part-time on nights. This allowed me to spend as much time as possible with Rebecca, whilst maintaining my midwifery practice. Three years later my son Jacob was born and our family was complete.

It was a strange thing being a midwife and having a baby, especially having worked in the neo-natal unit. You have to keep a sense of perspective and remember that most pregnancies end up with a straightforward birth. However, there is always a small part of your head and heart that lets your imagination run away with itself and expects the worst. I thankfully had two normal births and two healthy babies – with no small thanks to my midwife!

I came back to work when they were small and did a couple of nights a week. Unfortunately, unlike Ros, I'm not a good night person – although night duty is a marvellous place to gain experience. There's more scope to give care, and less interference from the routine rounds of the day. So I came off nights when my son was about three and got a job in parent education, where I could work regular, day-time hours. It was such a great job to have. Parent education classes give couples an opportunity to ask all those niggling questions they want answers to. You have to keep abreast of all the latest developments in labour and childbirth and I worked with a variety of different professionals and voluntary groups. Having worked part-time for a number of years supporting parents in all aspects of parent education, I was enticed back to full-time work when my daughter was fourteen and my son had started his first year at secondary school. It was a two-year project working in a small team including a health visitor, a community development worker and a play worker, adopting the government's Sure Start principles about early intervention to promote health and play. That was fascinating. It helped me to understand how services interact with families and how the midwifery dimension, that we think is so important, is just a drop in the ocean in women's lives. A mother is an individual, who sits within a family and within a community. We see the mother as an individual here, but they can be supported in a much broader way than just by the services they receive on the labour ward. Midwives have a great opportunity to develop a relationship with a mum and her family during the ante-natal period whilst she is pregnant. We can provide considerable encouragement in helping women to choose and adopt healthy lifestyle choices that will benefit themselves and their baby. Sometimes midwives working in the hospital only see the support they can offer whilst the mum is in labour or on the post-natal wards, but we have to be mindful that mums can be offered much broader and sustained support for the whole of their parenting. We are the gatekeepers to other services.

As a result of my job in the project, I applied for a senior midwifery manager post back in the maternity services. I was anxious that the work I had been involved in would continue to be supported and the benefits to some of our most vulnerable women would not be lost. When the opportunity then arose to apply for head of midwifery, I felt compelled to go for it. To lead a service that I am so proud of with such an amazing team is a privilege, and I am proud that it is the service that trained me as a midwife.

I have been married for twenty-eight years and my husband and family always come first. I would move heaven and earth for them. And this service is like my second family. I don't want to relinquish it to anyone else. We are a very passionate team, we get excited when things are going well and quite angry when things are unjust.

A while ago we had a special day to celebrate our successes. Two of our student midwives stood up to speak about what midwifery meant to them. I found the whole thing incredibly emotional and when asked to comment at the end of their presentation I wasn't able to as I'd been moved to tears. They were talking about their journey as student midwives and what a privilege it was to be looking after women. One was a mature student and was fulfilling a long-held dream. Hearing their impressions and thoughts about the profession they'd chosen was so inspiring. It's a marvellous thing to see new midwives coming through their training and understanding the wonderful partnership that can develop between the midwife and the pregnant woman. I see our role, alongside caring for mothers and babies, as supporting that introduction to family life. The transition from being individual people to being parents is such a change as well as a joy and we want to help them as much as we can.

We do socialise with each other outside of work – when we can find the time! One of the special things about working here is the sense of teamwork. You will often find that after a particularly stressful day or week, small groups of close colleagues will go out for a drink, or organise a trip to the pictures or theatre. We always try to have a lunch for new staff or when there are occasions to celebrate a job well done. There are some great cooks amongst us, as you could probably see from all the homemade cakes in the midwives' office! One of our midwives always makes special cakes for birthdays or staff who are leaving. Getting to know one another is an important part of daily work, understanding individual strengths helps us to work effectively as a team, providing the best care to women. It's important to have a sense of who we all are outside of work. I have to make decisions and I know that sometimes they're unpopular. Just because I'm head of midwifery it doesn't mean that my role is worth more than anyone else's. I'm not particularly hierarchical – everyone has a job to do and I'm part of the team. I'd be very disappointed if people felt I was aloof or remote. I like to talk to people and am happy that they come and talk to me when things aren't quite right. We all need each other for things to function properly and nobody is more important than anyone else. We're like a body, if we lose one part things don't work properly.

For somebody who had no career plan, I suppose my own rise has been rather a quick one. Every day I say to myself, 'Am I *really* a head of midwifery?' I still sometimes can't quite believe it.

2

FORTY BABIES TO GO!

It was a decision that I made when I was quite young, to become a midwife, but it's definitely not one I regret. Before I started the course I don't think anybody could actually have prepared me for the things I would have been doing, and you can read as much as you want but the best way to learn is to do it.

Marie, episode 6

ROS

The rules for midwives in training are very strict. Watch ten deliveries, then do ten with a trained midwife's hands on our hands, then do thirty deliveries ourselves witnessed by a trained midwife. New midwives get a lot of advice and guidance from their more experienced colleagues, which is a good job because some of the manoeuvres we had to get to grips with were pretty tricky. Some were even unintentionally comical . . .

I remember one of the sisters on labour ward was known as Sister Wiji, because no one could pronounce her full Sri Lankan name. She was absolutely lovely. When I first started working as a midwife one of the techniques to open up a woman's pelvis was to put her feet on our hips. I remember vividly trying to do that to help try to create a bigger space for the baby to come out. Every time the woman pushed, I ended up being pushed down the bed! Poor Sister Wiji had to push me back up the bed. If anyone who knew nothing about midwifery had come in and witnessed this bizarre scene, they would have wondered what on earth was going on! This procedure is no longer in use . . . for health and safety reasons!

During our training we alternated between time spent in the classroom learning theory with practical, hands-on time spent on the ward. Literally, hands on! As we progressed through the course, the ratio of clinical work to theory increased and we started to spend just one day a week in the classroom. I was delighted about this because I loved being in the thick of the action on the labour ward. We rotated time on the ward with time spent with women post-natally, ante-natally and in the community. There was a new intake of midwives every four months, so we saw a lot of new faces.

Our target was to deliver forty babies by the time we had finished our training, so we were always competing with other student midwives for deliveries. As students we didn't have a choice about which cases were assigned to us, and obviously we had no control over how long a labour would take. There were times that I got to the end of the shift and the baby of the woman I'd spent hours looking after in labour hadn't arrived. That was always hugely disappointing. Of course, labour takes as long as it takes and you can't hurry a baby up to coincide with the duration of your shift. But because as trainees it was so important to us to chalk up the necessary number of births, we were all desperate to deliver the baby of every woman we looked after. You'll often find student midwives staying late so that they can deliver the baby of the woman they've spent their shift looking after.

There used to be rules about which babies students could and couldn't deliver. If meconium was seen – a sign that the baby had opened its bowels and so might be in distress – we weren't allowed to do the delivery. Of course, now that I'm an experienced midwife, delivering babies is no longer a numbers game. We don't keep score, but the pleasure of delivering a baby never fades – particularly because when we're working alongside students, we have to let them deliver the babies so they can reach the target.

Students never know beforehand whether or not they'll be delivering their first baby – as I said, they are only allowed to deliver babies where everything is straightfor-ward. Labour can be unpredictable, and so we never knew until just before the birth whether or not we'd be delivering the baby. It meant that we didn't get nervous for days or hours ahead of a delivery, which was probably a good thing. By the time we were senior students we were allowed to do unsupervised deliveries; the midwife would stand outside, peeking through the venetian blind that covered the square of glass in the door to make sure we weren't committing any glaring errors. I remember performing one delivery with another student with one of the sisters observing me from outside the room. The delivery was very straightforward, but I was horrified to see that the baby came out a bit pale and shocked. It wasn't making a sound. We rubbed it with a towel which is often enough to make a baby go pink and start crying, but that didn't work so we had to take it outside the room to give it some oxygen.

My heart was racing and I was in a complete state of panic.

'What if the baby doesn't start crying? Have we done something terribly wrong?' I said to myself.

To my enormous relief, once the baby had been given the oxygen it turned a healthy shade of pink and produced a good, strong cry. The best sound in the world! We took it back into the room and proudly handed it to the mother. Afterwards the sister who'd been observing gave us feedback.

'Very nice delivery. I'm going to give you nine-and-a-half out of ten for it,' she said, smiling.

'What did we lose the half for?' I asked, puzzled.

'The look of sheer panic on your face when you realised the baby was going to need some resuscitation. Don't forget that the woman and whoever's with her looks to you for reassurance,' said the sister. 'The expression on your faces was telling that poor woman that there was something terribly wrong with her baby.'

Since then, I've really worked at exuding a sense of calmness and control however hair-raising a situation I find myself in. What I'm feeling underneath my cool, calm exterior is often another matter entirely. But even in the direst emergency, controlling your facial expression and tone of voice is vital.

Some students get their forty deliveries early on if they're particularly proactive. I was just relieved when I'd managed to do forty deliveries by the end of my training!

All in all, the midwifery course was very practical and the exam at the end of it was based on all the things I'd been doing over the last eighteen months, so it was relatively easy which was a relief. The first time I delivered a baby by myself, I knew that I'd broken through a crucial barrier. As a midwife, believing in your own skills and abilities is very important when it comes to putting into practice everything you've learned. And I soon realised that you never stop learning in this job. I feel I was a good midwife before I had my children, but after I'd given birth to all four of them, there was so much extra advice that I could offer, drawing on my own personal experiences. I remembered specific things I'd had problems with, and when I saw other women struggling at the same points in their labour, I could suggest things that had helped me.

With my first daughter, I needed forceps and an episiotomy. I had looked after other women who had had the same procedure, but until I had experienced it myself, I could not believe quite how painful it was. From then on, I was so much more sympathetic to other women who had to undergo that procedure. I was also better able to understand other common problems, like sore nipples from breastfeeding and the constant anxiety about every little thing the baby does or does not do. 'Is this normal?' 'Is that normal?' are phrases which are forever on the lips of new mums, and it's very important to help put their minds at rest.

There is such a thing as a textbook delivery: the woman starts with mild contractions that gradually get stronger, until the baby's head rotates through the pelvis and more or less delivers itself. And during and after the birth both mother and baby are fine. Many women do give birth in that way. However, as a midwife you see many, many births and inevitably not all of them are as beautifully straightforward and successful as the textbooks predict. It's surprising just how many things don't go to plan during labour, although thankfully many of the problems that arise can be

put right very quickly and don't adversely affect the outcome for the mother and her baby. Some babies don't
rotate, or get stuck mid-rotation, others are breech. And
while many women go into labour spontaneously, others
don't and the process needs to be kick-started using drugs
to stimulate contractions.

Not long after I'd qualified, I remember one woman
arriving in the labour ward around 6 a.m. She had been in
pain for hours at home, but her husband worked nights and
she had waited for him to get home to bring her in.
Although she didn't know it, she had had an abruption –
where the placenta separates from the lining of the uterus
before labour. She was bleeding very heavily, which is often
a sign that this has happened. The loss of so much blood had
made her extremely poorly. Sadly, the baby didn't survive
and she was in a critical condition after it was delivered. I
can still see her poor husband standing beside her, crying.
Both of them had been so looking forward to the birth and
nobody expects a tragedy like this to happen.

It was the first time I had seen so much blood. It was
dripping onto the floor and we were constantly mopping it
up. I didn't realise there could be so much blood inside one
body. I had never encountered that level of despair in the
delivery room before. The baby is the prize at the end of a
long pregnancy and a hard labour, but in that room there
was no prize, only grief. There's little that can be said to
comfort parents in such a situation. It's important to respect

their privacy, give them proper time to grieve and offer them as much support as possible.

A cord prolapse is another problem that I've encountered from time to time – this is when the cord comes into the open cervix in front of the baby. It is then squeezed by the baby, cutting off the flow of oxygen from the cord to the baby, a situation which could lead to death or long-term damage to the baby. This is a real emergency, and the woman needs to be rushed straight down to theatre for an emergency Caesarean. It's something that happens suddenly and unpredictably, one of those dramatic moments where the midwife presses the emergency buzzer and the room suddenly fills with medical personnel.

The baby's heartbeat dropping is a clue that the cord has prolapsed. It is vital that we protect the baby by placing our hand inside the woman's vagina to hold the head up off the cord, so that the oxygen supply can be maintained until she gets to theatre. The only way to do this is for the midwife to get up on the bed with the woman as she is rushed to theatre.

One time I arrived in theatre in that position, with my hand inside the woman's body to keep the cord separate until the baby had been delivered. Sterile drapes were put over the woman's lower half, which is routine practice when she is being prepared for a Caesarean. Of course, that meant I was completely covered by the drapes too. After a while the doctors, engrossed in what they were doing, seemed to have forgotten that I was still hidden between the woman's legs. Next thing I knew, I was whacked over the head with a retractor, one of the surgical implements.

'Excuse me! Don't forget I'm still in here!' I squealed, not quite sure whether to laugh or cry. Thankfully, the emergency delivery went smoothly – both mother and baby were fine and I clambered out from under the sterile drapes just a little worse for wear. There was so much adrenaline pumping while I was on the operating table with the woman that I didn't really notice anything else – not even head injuries. And there was such a huge sense of relief afterwards when everything turned out fine that getting hit on the head seemed like a small price to pay. Needless to say, we all had a good laugh about it afterwards!

One of the things I really love about my job is the respect that all the different members of the medical team have for each other's role and knowledge. We all work together so well. I'm included in discussions with doctors and others, and they listen to my opinions. I think I'm in a really privileged place and I never take that for granted. Working in an atmosphere of mutual respect has got to be the best possible environment to work in.

We learnt about a whole range of scenarios in the class-room before we were allowed to look after women. Some of the more serious conditions that can arise in labour, like cord prolapse and abruption, are thankfully rare. But although we're trained to deal with emergencies like these, there's no substitute for experience and the best way to become a competent, capable midwife is just to get out there and do the job.

MARIA

The midwifery course I did was for people who were already qualified nurses. There were a smaller group of us than there had been on my nursing course, which was nice. I had quite a lot of work experience as I'd already worked in the neo-natal unit. Some of my course-mates eventually returned to nursing afterwards, because they really didn't enjoy midwifery. Midwifery is a calling, and either you're right for it or you're not.

One of the first things we learnt on the course was that when a midwife does a vaginal examination, she uses the first and second fingers of her right hand. She uses her fingers to assess the birth canal, the size of the pelvis, the dilation of the cervix and the position of the baby's head. You will often see a midwife describe her findings by rotating or wiggling her fingers, as though she is remembering what she felt through her fingers. One of my fellow students only had half of one of the fingers on her right hand. Nobody noticed for a while, but then one student piped up, 'Do vaginal examinations *have* to be done with the right hand?'

'Yes. After you've palpated you stand on that side of the mother,' replied the tutor, looking surprised that anyone should consider deviating from the norm. The tutor then glanced at the student with the missing half-finger and looked perplexed. It was agreed in the end that, just this once, this student could use her left hand instead. The whole thing did cause an unbelievable amount of fuss! We had a laugh about the tutor's reaction afterwards, because to us students it seemed like such a minor thing to get worked up about. Really there's absolutely no reason at all why a midwife shouldn't do an examination with her left hand rather than her right. It was simply a case of 'that's how we've always done things and that's how we'll continue to do them'.

I've always considered my midwifery training to be a real privilege. Because I'd worked at the neo-natal unit I never felt like a naive student, more like a colleague of the midwives. I didn't mind going back to the classroom, but some of the qualified nurses didn't like the feeling of being a student again and couldn't get used to the change of pace of midwifery compared with nursing. We looked at diagrams in the classroom and practised delivering dummy babies. After delivering a few dolls, the mechanics of birth suddenly started to make sense to me. We learned about how the baby rotates into the pelvis and began to understand exactly what the baby's journey from the womb into the world entails. Knowing what's going on inside the woman's body even though you can't actually see anything gives you a sense of real understanding as a midwife.

Until I began my midwifery training, I had absolutely no idea about just what happens when a baby makes its journey out of a woman's body. A woman's body is a pretty extraordinary feat of design. During the first stage of labour, the baby rotates into the right position. The baby tucks its head in so that it's ready to negotiate the pelvis during the second, pushing stage of labour. The top of the uterus contracts down on the baby's bottom and legs, propelling it downwards towards the cervix. Resistance from the pelvic-floor muscle causes the baby to rotate into the right position to continue its journey. The baby extends its head upwards as it emerges from under its mother's pubic bone. The shoulders rotate so that they're lying in the widest part of the pelvis. The top shoulder slips beneath the woman's pubic bone followed by the bottom shoulder and the rest of the body. Amazing stuff!

I'd never delivered a baby during my nursing training and I was absolutely terrified of doing it for the first time as a midwife. The way it worked was first to watch other midwives delivering babies, then to do some with the midwife's hands over your hands and then do the whole thing solo. I always used to think that the women who allowed us students to practise on them were very brave and generous spirited.

The first time I delivered a baby by myself was with another student midwife. The qualified midwife who was supervising checked up on us by standing on the other side of the door and peeping in at us through the glass panel. The woman who was in labour was really lovely. It was her second birth and she really did 'crack on' quickly. That's the slang we use for a woman making progress in labour. She had planned to have an epidural but her labour accelerated too quickly for the anaesthetist to administer one. My student colleague and I agreed that I would conduct the birth and she would receive the baby. Her partner was very anxious about the fact that a couple of students were in charge.

'So you're not qualified yet?' he asked, nervously.

'No, but there's a very experienced midwife watching us outside the door and I promise you we've done all our training,' I said, calmly, trying to sound as reassuring as I could although I was actually extremely nervous. Thankfully, everything went smoothly and we all breathed a collective sigh of relief when a lovely, healthy baby was born.

My whole training was very positive. I'm sure that part of it was that I'd spent a lot of time on labour ward previously, through the neo-natal unit, so it felt like home already. One thing I did find a bit frustrating was that though our learning was very up-to-date and evidence-based, some of the clinicians I was working alongside were not quite so ready or willing to change. Some clinicians wanted to do what they'd always done because that had always worked for them, but we completed our course all fired up and determined to change the world, putting into practice what we had learnt. It's a bit like our midwifery tutor and her preference for the right hand, I suppose – a reluctance to try something new or different.

There was a great reluctance to consider water births when I first qualified. It's now really common for women to get into the pool and the warm water can really help them get through labour. When pool births were fairly new, about twenty years ago, Julia Clark, now our Midwifery Matron, cared for a young woman who seemed really keen to have a pool birth. Julia had spent some time running the water to make sure that it was the right temperature and depth to keep the expectant mum warm. Julia helped her into the pool, in between strong contractions and with the help of her partner. But within seconds of her sitting in the water, she stood back up and stepped out of the pool, dripping.

'My mother didn't want me to have a pool birth, I can't go through with it,' she said. 'I'm really sorry, but I just keep hearing my mother say that it's not right to have a baby in water, and what if it drowns?' Of course, the young mum had already been told that this wouldn't happen, but she just couldn't relax with her mother's voice inside her head. So out of the water she came, and went on to have a lovely active labour, but a 'dry land' birth. It's funny how a woman's mother can exert a particularly strong influence over her when she's in labour.

Pool births can be absolutely lovely, but the baby needs to be delivered into the water to keep warm and it is an acquired skill to support a mum birthing in water. The baby is brought to the surface of the water before it takes its first breath. Julia looked after another mum who suddenly stood up just as the baby was being born, and Julia struggled to catch the baby before it plunged back into the pool! Luckily the dad realised what was about to happen and helped Julia hold onto the baby and prevent it from diving back into the water.

Julia recalled another memorable occasion where a baby who was born in the pool brought her arms forward and stretched upwards, emerging out of the water on her own – just like Esther Williams!

One particular incident from my training has always stayed with me. After a baby is delivered, the cord is cut, the baby is handed over to its mother and an injection of Syntometrine, and oxytoxic drug, is given in the leg to help the uterus contract. This helps the uterus to contract, which causes the placenta to separate from the uterine wall. Often the first sign of this is when the umbilical cords lengthens visibly on the outside. At this point the midwife knows it is possible to delivery the placenta safely. But with one woman I was looking after this didn't happen, as is sometimes the way. The midwife who was teaching me that day told me to wait for a few minutes longer to see if it came down of its own accord. When it didn't, she put her hand on mine and yanked the cord, breaking it in the process. She called out to a passing medic, 'The little mid-wife just snapped the cord. The mum will have to go to theatre!' I felt humiliated for something that wasn't my fault. The mum needed to go to surgery to have the placenta removed. It might not have been necessary if we had waited for a while, although it is also possible that the outcome might have been the same. I'll never know!

I was upset to have been blamed for something that I didn't consider to be my fault. I was young and inexperienced, but I vowed then that if I didn't know how to do something I would hold my hand up, admit the gaps in my knowledge and ask for help rather than blaming someone else.

One of the nicest things about our job is delivering a woman's baby and then seeing her again, a year or two later, when she comes back to give birth to her second child. This happened to Julia, and ended up with a very embarrassing moment for her.

'I was delivering a second baby for a woman whose first baby I had also delivered,' she told me. 'Everything went very well and she gave birth to a beautiful baby. The atmosphere was calm and peaceful and I felt a real connection with the woman because I'd delivered both her babies. After the baby was born, I delivered the placenta and that all went smoothly, too. But to my horror, as I was about to put the placenta in a dish close to the bed, it slid out of my hands and landed right in the middle of the bag of pristine baby clothes she had lovingly packed and brought to the hospital! Needless to say, they were far *less* pristine after they were splattered with blood and other fluids from the placenta. Fortunately, the woman forgave me, but the peaceful atmosphere we had all been enjoying evaporated rather quickly.'

Some incidents that happen on the ward quickly pass into legend. One of our student midwives thought she had lost a baby's heartbeat and naturally started to panic. The mother had had an epidural, was feeling very relaxed and couldn't feel a thing. Various staff rushed into the room, primed to deal with a major emergency. As one of the staff lifted up the sheet that covered her to do a vaginal examination, she found to her amazement that the baby had slid out unnoticed and lay nestled between the mother's legs. Because the woman was completely numb from the epidural she couldn't feel that there was a baby lying in between her thighs!

'I imagine *that's* why you couldn't find the heartbeat,' said one of the doctors, raising an eyebrow at the mortified student.

As you can imagine, the story went all round the hospital and caused a great deal of hilarity. It took the poor girl a while to live it down, and she cringed every time someone said, 'Found any babies in the bed recently?'

Another of my favourite stories is from way back when

student midwives had to wear little white caps. One midwife's fell off, just as she was delivering a baby and you can imagine where it landed – right on the baby's head! It looked for all the world like the baby had emerged from the womb complete with a natty little hat!

Midwifery is quite literally a case of what you see is what you get. It really teaches you about what is of value in life and what isn't. What matters most is the welcome you get from people. Julia did two post-natal visits: one to a very wealthy couple who lived in a mansion surrounded by electronic gates; the other was to a new mum who lived in a humble council house. The welcome was far warmer from the woman who lived in the council house; she made the midwife feel she was doing something worthwhile. With the wealthy couple she felt she was simply a hindrance. Appearances and outer trappings don't mean much in our line of work. What really counts are the essential qualities that people have. Birth is a very true and raw process and midwives are good at seeing through hypocrisy and insincerity.

A happy and hopefully healthy mum and a healthy baby is the midwife's reward for the care we provide and when we forge a genuine bond with the mother, it makes the whole experience even more rewarding.

3

THE MYSTERIES OF BIRTH

*Ask anybody who has run the London marathon;
everybody faces their own wall and I think it is
undersold that labour is a huge physical challenge
and with a huge physical challenge comes the
mental wall, 'I can't do it, I can't do it. This isn't
going to work.' But eventually, with a bit of coaxing
and support, women will get through.*

Dominique, episode 3

ROS

As midwives we get to know every detail about pregnancy
and childbirth. Everyone is familiar with the old wives' tales
about the shape of women's bumps when they're pregnant,
and whether a certain shape means that the woman will
have a girl or a boy. I can tell you that there is absolutely no
scientific proof for any of these theories, but it doesn't stop

people from guessing! And as for tying your wedding ring to a piece of string and dangling it over your bump . . .

It's true, though, that women will have a different shape depending on how many pregnancies they've had. During the first pregnancy the stomach muscles are more taut, and sad to say they do slacken with subsequent pregnancies. Unless of course you're a supermodel or an elite athlete like Paula Radcliffe, who seem to have eternally youthful stomach muscles which ping back into washboard position within days of giving birth! Don't you just love them?

Women do have bumps of all different sizes though, and that can be related to their own size and fitness, or where they come from. Asian women tend to have smaller babies than white women, for example, so it's important to recognise what's normal for each individual woman. What matters is that the woman is eating well, has a properly functioning placenta and enough fluid around the baby.

Some bumps can look bigger than they are because the baby is surrounded by a lot of fluid. Women who are slim, having their first baby and do a lot of exercise often don't look pregnant until they're quite far along. And larger women may not look very pregnant at all. When women arrive at the hospital in labour, having only just realised they're pregnant, they tend to be the larger women.

Obesity is a problem for an increasing number of pregnant women, as are cardiac conditions and smoking-related health problems. Larger women may develop gestational diabetes, and it can be difficult for the midwife to assess the size and position of the baby or even do a scan. Women with entrenched drug addictions are in the minority, but there are quite a lot of women who have used drugs recreationally and some continue to use drugs in this way throughout their pregnancy, which we would obviously discourage. If they are living in an environment where others are using, it can be extremely hard to give up and peer pressure can encourage them to continue using.

We try our best to disseminate positive health messages to women when we give them their ante-natal care. The healthier they are, the better it is for them and their baby and the better they're likely to cope with the demands of giving birth.

It's fascinating to see how women change in labour. For many, childbirth is the only time in their life when they become more primal. One woman came in recently looking so immaculate and well groomed – she didn't have a hair out of place and I wondered how she would manage as her labour progressed. As her contractions strengthened, she became more and more dishevelled. Her well-groomed exterior fell away and she embraced her inner, primal self. She completely surrendered herself to her instinct.

I've noticed that professional women who are usually totally in control of their lives seem to cope less well with the messier side of birth – the explosion of bodily fluids! –

than others who are more prepared to go with the flow. Sometimes teachers struggle with the unpredictability of labour, because they are so used to control and don't like relinquishing it. There are ways, though, for the mother to take some control back during labour. The National Childbirth Trust teach pregnant women certain rhythmic chants, like 'The Grand Old Duke of York' for example, to help to get them breathe in time with their contractions. Some women might choose some other song or mantra, or some might unleash a few choice swear words! Others focus on one particular part of the room. Any techniques to help women to stay in control during labour can be really useful.

Giving birth to a baby is an amazing physical achievement. When a woman has pushed for an hour-and-a-half, or two hours, she becomes completely and utterly exhausted, but miraculously, just when all her physical energy has faded away, the mental energy kicks in and ensures that she keeps going just that little bit longer. The midwife's role in encouraging a woman to keep going and keep pushing is a vital one: birth is as much a psychological process as a physical one.

We come across so many diverse situations in our line of work. Of course there is enormous joy involved in bringing a new life into the world, but even when a healthy, bouncing baby is born and the mother is fine, there can still be sad stories. Just recently a woman told me that her partner, the baby's father, had left her for another man during her pregnancy. It was so sad to see her all alone during the labour and with no one there to celebrate the birth with her.

If women are in a position to talk during their labour, they may confide various bits of information to us, something they're at pains to keep hidden at other times in their life when they have more control over their bodies and their emotions – perhaps how they *really* feel about their mother-in-law or another relative. But while some women open up and tell you their life story, others remain tight lipped and you find out little more than their name, date of birth and how dilated their cervix is.

We'll often get a woman coming into the ward in the early stages of labour because she's not coping at home ... or more likely, her partner isn't coping and he doesn't know what to do to help her any more! But it's often the case that the woman's labour may not be advanced enough for her to be at hospital at that point. Often a detailed conversation over the phone can prevent this happening, which benefits both us and the women – if women come in too early, they have to return home and we have to fill out lots of paperwork recording their brief visit to the labour ward.

One of the hardest things to deal with is when people are demanding, aggressive and abusive. Sometimes it's because they're frightened and stressed, but sometimes it's because that's just the way they are. I delivered one baby using a ventouse – a sort of suction cup that helps the baby out if it gets a bit stuck, which I'm trained to use – and I gave the woman an episiotomy. She was surprised that it was me and not the doctor who delivered her baby. One of my colleagues spent a long time afterwards explaining and pointing out that there hadn't been any complications. Sometimes women don't realise that the midwife's role is expanding to include procedures which might previously have been performed exclusively by doctors.

We often find that with the fast-paced life people lead these days, they sometimes get impatient if a baby doesn't seem to be arriving quickly enough. When things are going slowly they'll demand, 'I want a Caesarean now!' We have to explain that there's no clinical indication that such a procedure is needed. But a rational response doesn't always go down well in the throes of labour.

The arrival of the epidural has transformed the labour process for both midwives and women. Epidurals mean more monitoring, more machines and less opportunity for the midwife to encourage the woman to work with her body to push the baby out. It's a much more technical job than traditional labour. They make things easier for the midwife in one way because the woman's stress levels have reduced so you don't have to give as much encouragement and emotional support, but it's more difficult for us because the labour becomes more high-tech and more can go wrong. There are more machines to monitor. But because the woman is calmer and pain-free, she sometimes wants to talk, especially if the labour is a long one. If the midwife and the woman click, we can have some lovely chats.

If a woman has an epidural during the night, of course you have to be there but it can be quite a soporific experience for the midwife if she falls asleep. I often find myself marching up and down the room, desperately trying to stay awake! As you can imagine, the anaesthetists are the most popular people on the wards because they can transform the labour experience and remove all the pain. But the epidurals they administer don't always work, and we have to deal with a woman's disappointment if the pain doesn't vanish. Although the anaesthetists are very well loved, there's quite a lot of pressure on them to do the epidural right and do it quickly.

MARIA

Midwives tend to develop a preference for a particular aspect of the job. Some love to combine working in the community with delivering babies in the hospital, home or birth centre and others like to care for women who have more complicated medical or obstetric needs and work predominantly in the hospital. I loved looking after women that were aiming for a normal birth. There is a real sense of achievement in working with a mum, helping her to cope with the discomfort of labour, encouraging her to try different positions, talking her through a contraction, coaxing her to relax in between the bouts of pain. Just being with her and responding to her needs as she approaches the moment of birth.

When a woman doesn't have an epidural, there's much more work for the midwife to do in terms of encouraging the woman through her contractions. There are different observations that need doing because the woman requires close monitoring as she is having continuous pain relief. Observing all the machines when a woman's had an epidural can be really monotonous, especially on night duty. The woman and her partner may well fall asleep and we midwives are left sitting in a dark, dim room, doing observations and listening to the baby's heartbeat and acting as guardians of a safe labour. We have to provide one-to-one care, so we're alone in that quiet room. It can feel much more rewarding helping a mother who has had a bit more of a struggle to give birth without an epidural, although it can be frustrating if that labour doesn't progress.

The outcome of a birth can often change if the woman is able to move around. We can look at the way the baby's lying and try to find the best position for the woman to get into so that the baby comes down into the pelvis the right way, which is really important. For example, keeping upright is a fantastic way to get the baby to turn and go down into the pelvis. But that isn't an option when a woman has an epidural and is stuck on her back in bed, although we do encourage changing position, including swapping from one side to the other.

Women can set themselves unrealistic goals before they go into labour. For example, one woman told a midwife that she didn't want any 'negative energy' in the room and that she wasn't to mention the word 'pain'. Rather an idealistic approach and not necessarily matched by the reality of giving birth to a child! The truth is that childbirth *is* often painful, because a woman needs to have pretty strong contractions in order to push a baby out. There's no way round that one. But you have to remember that it's a different kind of pain from that of an illness, and there's a happy reason for it. It's also pain that can be managed, and that the woman knows will end.

After a woman's had one baby, the pushing stage is easier. It's like blowing up a balloon – much harder the first time you do it. Having said that, women do tend to get more aches and pains with babies after the first one, because the muscles aren't as tight – they loosen after the first pregnancy and after that, well, things are never quite the same again! The pregnancy hormones also help to loosen the joints. We often see a thing called Symphesis Pubis Dysfunction. At the front of the pelvis there's cartilage down the middle and that often loosens during pregnancy, so there's movement in the pelvis. It allows just that little bit of extra give to allow the baby to come through, but it can cause pain in the pregnancy. As the pregnancy progresses, women sometimes say they can feel the bits of the pelvis grinding and moving against each other. It's a common complication of pregnancy, like heartburn and morning sickness, but it can be really uncomfortable. I remember when I was pregnant and experiencing morning sickness, some people would say 'it's in your mind' and make light of it. Believe me, when it's happening to you, it's quite real and very unpleasant!

Women sometimes go into pregnancy thinking they'll sail straight through it, and a lot are quite surprised that it's uncomfortable and causes pain. But think of a big baby pushing against all your other organs – they get squashed to the back and the side, and you have to expect a certain amount of discomfort. It does help to allay some anxieties when we explain that the baby presses on a lot of nerves.

We find that women tend to have less chance to rest in their second or third (or fourth, or fifth …) pregnancies than they do first time round. In the first pregnancy everyone's excited, but subsequent ones aren't such a novelty and people aren't fussing around you. It can feel much harder – particularly if you're looking after young children, too.

In the majority of cases the second labour is quicker

than the first, but there are always people who disprove that. Because the cervix has dilated once before, it will generally dilate more quickly in later labours and a second baby will tend to come out more quickly. A woman who had a forceps delivery in her first labour, or some other complication, is likely to feel anxious about a second birth. These women often need a lot of reassurance and encouragement, but just because something happened first time round doesn't mean that it will happen again. Everybody has got a different anatomy, some women stretch better than others – it depends on the size and position of the baby's head. But just because a woman had stitches and an episiotomy for one baby, for example, it doesn't mean she'll have to have the same experience with all her children.

We midwives have a lot of our own theories about pregnancy and labour. One of them is about women having their third babies – we often find that third labours can be a bit awkward. The first labour tends to be quite long, the second shorter, and with the third women can often get false alarms, think that they're in labour and then find that their contractions suddenly stop.

It's sometimes very difficult for women who arrive in an advanced state of labour, huffing and puffing, to work with their body to control the pain of their contractions. It becomes a vicious circle – the pain makes their bodies rigid in between contractions. If they can relax between contractions, it makes the whole process much easier. But if, instead of using the time between contractions to recover from the last contraction, they are bracing themselves for the next wave of pain and this only adds to their fear and discomfort.

Our job is to try to get them to stay as calm and relaxed as possible, to understand how their body is responding to being in labour and how to work with it. The more a woman tenses up, the more painful things get. If she tries to let the contraction work its way through her body like a rippling wave, it's going to be much more effective at pushing the baby out and making the pain more manageable. When a woman has got herself into a cycle of fear it can be a real challenge to break that cycle and get her back in tune with the rhythms of her contractions. Reassuring her and showing her that we can help her to regain control gives her confidence. It's also important for us as midwives to remember that everybody's pain threshold is different and that, objectively speaking, some labours *are* more painful than others. All these factors have a huge bearing on how the woman copes with labour.

When it comes to the point when a woman is ready to push her baby out, a lot of it is down to mental attitude. Midwives often say to women, 'I know you're tired and it's been a long time, but this is the last bit. You can do it, really you can.' We don't want to falsely encourage the woman and say the baby's nearly here when it's not, but it's important to offer the maximum encouragement while remaining honest and realistic.

We hear these stories of women who are 'too posh to push' and opt for an elective Caesarean. They don't like the idea of puffing and panting their way through labour, and are worried about the damage that a vaginal birth might do to their sex lives. It may be possible to book elective Caesareans at private hospitals, simply because a woman prefers it, but it certainly doesn't work that way on the NHS. Caesareans are performed on the basis of clinical need, *not* convenience. This is for the safety of the mother and baby.

Sometimes women come in really disturbed and in unbearable pain and can't believe they're only one centimetre dilated, while for others that early stage of labour barely makes them flinch. If a woman becomes sleep deprived, she tends not to cope as well with pain as her energy reserves are drained, so it's important that she gets as much rest as she can, whilst she can. Women are free to make as much noise as they want during labour, of course, but it takes a lot of energy to scream and that energy can be put to better use to focus on getting through the contractions. When women scream it usually means they've lost control and they're in distress, which doesn't help labour or with the pushing process in the second stage of labour. At this point we try to make eye contact to help the woman get things back under control by the time the next contraction comes. But everybody copes with labour pain in a different way. Women from certain cultures – for example many of the women we look after from Somalia and Sudan – are particularly quiet in labour. Some women accept the pain more than others.

Pushing sounds like a very straightforward business, but it's important to focus on pushing from the right part of the body. Basically, all the pushing has to be powered into the woman's bottom. Some women are inhibited from doing this because they're worried that they might empty their bowels, but really they just have to get past that and get on with the task in hand. If a woman does empty her bowels, it just means that she's pushing in the right place. It's nothing to be ashamed of.

Women do get an instinctive urge to push during the second stage of labour when the baby is moving down into the pelvis. At this stage the woman often just needs to hear the midwife's voice and not the voices of her loved ones, because she's at a crucial point and shouldn't push at the wrong time. At this point it's particularly important to encourage women to tune into their bodies. If women do too much yelling and screaming through a contraction, all the energy is coming out through their mouth instead of focusing on the lower part of their body where it's needed.

At one time women who had epidurals couldn't feel any pushing urge or sensation but epidurals now are lighter than they used to be. However, we have to give more guidance to women who have had epidurals and alert them to the fact that they're having a contraction – otherwise we might end up in the same situation as our poor student midwife and her surprise delivery! There are lots of different factors involved with pushing. If a woman has a quicker labour, she'll be a lot fresher and will have more energy for the final part. I do feel sorry for the women who've pushed all the way through a long labour and are overwhelmed with exhaustion before they've pushed the baby out.

I remember one woman coming in in very strong labour with her first baby. She had an urge to go to the loo and said she could feel something whilst sat there. It was the baby's head. She was helped back into the delivery room next door and it was suggested she stood up leaning slightly over the bed and had her baby standing up.

As this baby was born, its head delivered beautifully and slowly. The baby turned its head gently to get its shoulders into the right position to come out. The young woman was very controlled about the whole thing. As the body started to deliver, the baby gently poked out one arm, then the other and the baby was gently supported as the rest of its body was born. The midwife did very little, and it was so amazing to see this baby deliver itself so beautifully. As soon as the mum held her lovely baby in her arms, all the stress and exhaustion of the birth vanished.

One of the mysteries of childbirth is that women age ten years when they're in labour because they're in so much pain, but miraculously that extra decade slips off their faces as soon as the baby has been born.

4

MANUAL ACROBATICS AND OTHER CHALLENGES

Hang on, I've just got an ambulance at my desk, darling ... no, not the actual *ambulance at my desk ...*

Nancy, episode 3

ROS

Midwives operate 'blind' to a certain extent, because of course we can't see what the baby's doing when it's still inside the woman. So we have to employ a range of other techniques, such as listening and feeling, to get the most accurate picture of what's going on. Babies are relatively big things that have to be manoeuvred out of pretty tight spaces inside a woman's body, so the more techniques we can employ to help free babies that have got a bit stuck on their journey, the less likely it is that she will need to have an emergency Caesarean to get the baby out.

Women sometimes ask us how we manage to make such precise declarations about how many centimetres a woman's cervix is dilated. Well, here's a trade secret ... although it all sounds terribly exact, to be honest we can only offer educated guesses and each midwife's educated guess might be slightly different. If I can get one finger into a woman's cervix, then she's one centimetre dilated; two fingers is two centimetres; two fingers spread apart is three centimetres. Beyond four centimetres, you have to run your fingers round the edge of the cervix and work out how much cervix is left around the outside. Sometimes the cervix is very rigid and sometimes it's very stretchy, so it's important not to push it too far open or the woman will appear to be more dilated than she actually is. When the woman is ten centimetres dilated, the cervix has been totally pushed back.

So if a few midwives examined the same woman, one after the other, I can guarantee they wouldn't all say she was the same number of centimetres dilated.

While midwives are highly trained and very experienced, instinct and intuition are really important parts of our job. We have to be in tune with the women and with what's happening to their bodies in labour, and that helps us to support them. One of our navigational skills is working out what position the baby's head is in by feeling it carefully before it comes out. A baby's head bones are not fused – there's a diamond-shaped fontanel at the front of the head and triangular one at the back. The diamond-shaped fontanel is bigger and usually softer than the triangular one. By feeling the baby's head gently using these two clues, we can work out what's going on and what position the baby's in. One midwife I know, Lorna Bird, got the shock of her life when she was feeling inside a woman for the baby's head. Unbeknown to her, the baby had lifted its arm and its hand was resting on its head. As Lorna felt around the head, the baby grabbed her hand with its tiny fingers – I don't know who got more of a shock – the woman, the midwife or the baby!

Once the baby is delivered, we give an injection into the muscle to help expel the placenta. The majority of women have this injection and usually the placenta will deliver within ten minutes. If it hasn't happened after fifteen minutes we do a gentle internal examination to try to locate it inside the woman. Sometimes when we put our fingers inside the vagina, we can feel that the cervix has gone into spasm and closed too soon before the placenta has been expelled. A full bladder can stop the placenta coming out so we encourage the woman to empty her bladder and we might put her on a hormone drip to make her contract more strongly in the hope of expelling it. Sometimes inserting a finger inside the woman, hooking it into the edge of the placenta and getting her to push while I'm pulling gets it out.

Sometimes the placenta doesn't come out because it

hasn't separated from the wall of the uterus, which can cause bleeding. If the woman is bleeding we need to get the placenta out quickly. Generally if it's not out within an hour the woman will be taken down to theatre so that it can be removed surgically.

Like everything else associated with childbirth, placentas come in all shapes, sizes and textures. If a woman is overdue it can get a bit gritty with bits of calcium marbled through it. Most look plump and healthy, but smokers' placentas are often a bit lumpy as the smoking can affect blood flow and adversely affect its quality. We always try to encourage women to cut out or at least reduce their smoking in pregnancy, but it doesn't always work. I've noticed over the years that the women who've just had Caesarean sections or a particularly difficult labour but are *still* desperate to get out of bed are usually smokers. Some women beg to go outside to get their nicotine fix as soon as the placenta has been delivered!

I have also seen quite a few women bring in Tupperware pots to take their placentas home either to cook them or bury them ...

Every once in a while we get to perform a nifty manoeuvre which can prevent a woman being rushed to theatre. I remember being called in to help a midwife, because although the woman she was looking after had very strong contractions, there was no sign of the baby's head. The woman hadn't had an epidural and although it must have been very painful for her, she allowed me to do an internal examination to find out what position the baby's head was in. Alarm bells began to ring straight away – I could feel the baby's brow and the ridge of its nose. As I had suspected, the head was the wrong way round. The back of the head is designed to be squeezed on its way out of the mother's body, but you can't squash the bony bit of the face and the front of the head. When the baby is in this position it's known as a brow presentation. Babies in this position often get stuck and the usual solution is to perform an emergency Caesarean.

The woman was doing so well and it seemed a shame to put her through a Caesarean when everything else apart from the position of the baby's head was normal. I decided to try something before alerting the theatre team.

'Okay, next contraction I don't want you to push,' I said. With my fingers I managed to carefully push the baby's head upwards a bit. As I nudged it, it turned and flexed and moved into the right position for a normal vaginal delivery. I felt absolutely elated. I had never done anything like that before – the mother and baby were safe and the mother had avoided having a Caesarean with the associated risks and long recovery time. It was hugely satisfying. The other midwife looked at me and said, 'How on earth did you manage to do that?'

'I don't know, I've never done it before,' I admitted. 'I think there was a fair bit of luck involved. The woman was really cooperative and there was room in her pelvis for me to feel around and reposition the head.' All credit to her that she allowed me to do that. A lot of women wouldn't have tolerated that without an epidural.

Childbirth is such an amazing thing. I've seen babies lying inside their mother in completely the wrong position with their back against their mother's back all the time that the mother is pushing. Yet, literally as soon as the baby hits the perineum its head does a 180 degree spin round to put itself into the right position to be born. Getting onto all fours is very good for women who have a baby whose back is lying against their back. But some women feel too self-conscious to stick their bottom in the air!

A natural birth is when the woman pushes the baby out herself. I have a real respect for women who can do that, especially if the labour has been long and the woman has had to dig really deep into her energy reserves. A ventouse delivery is when a suction device is used to help deliver a baby who has got a bit stuck. I'm trained to do this kind of delivery and use the ventouse to guide the baby round a bend, mid-pelvis, where it's become wedged. Once the baby is round the bend and starting to crown, I don't do very much pulling at all. I'm guiding and the woman is pushing the baby out the rest of the way. The potential for maternal trauma using the ventouse is far less than a Caesarean, and there's a great sense of achievement after using it successfully in a delivery. The fewer invasive techniques we can use the better. We don't attach drips and wires and monitors to women willy nilly, but of course there are times when we must do it.

Babies emerge from the womb in all shapes and sizes. Some are beautiful with perfect, delicately shaped features while others look more like little Sumo wrestlers. When all of my children were born my mother-in-law took one look at them, even the girls, and declared that they looked like her father, a man we referred to as 'granddad Bradbury'. Some newborns are, quite frankly, less than beautiful, although they usually blossom later on. The best way to get out of a potentially tricky situation if the newborn isn't a beauty is to beam and say, 'Ooh, he looks just like you!'

MARIA

Part of the midwife's role is to try to build up a rapid rapport with a woman and her birth partner if she hasn't met them before. This can sometimes be a real challenge. A midwife knows that during labour she will be entering into a partnership that needs to be based on trust and confidence, because of the intimacy of the birth experience that she will be involved in with the mother. Every midwife will enter into this relationship hoping to be liked and to find a way that will her earn the respect and comradeship she will need to ensure the woman's experience is the best it can be. Of course there are occasions when the woman and the midwife allocated to her don't always get along. Or the woman's partner and the midwife may not take to each other – that's just part of human nature. We can't expect to always care for women that we like. But it's important to remain professional at all times, even though that can sometimes be hard on a twelve-hour shift. There are many challenges in this job and one of the less pleasant things we have to deal with is rudeness and aggressive behaviour.

Labour and childbirth are extremely stressful times and often provoke behaviour that people wouldn't normally exhibit. Often this happens because of fear, anger or frustration. Midwives will try to get to the bottom of what might have caused the outburst or problem but sometimes it's not possible. As head of midwifery I can be called on to try and resolve episodes of conflict that the midwives who are just trying to do their job find hard to deal with. Often it boils down to a misunderstanding or lack of communication. I try to remember that I am the professional and the person in front of me is likely to need my support even though they are not going about it in a pleasant way. Sometimes it's not possible to find a way to diffuse the situation and in order to protect the other women, families and staff, we have to use security. Fundamentally we cannot allow abusive and aggressive behaviour towards staff. Midwifery, even more than nursing, is a predominantly female profession and at times we can feel intimidated.

One of my staff had to deal with a man who was drunk. His girlfriend had just given birth and was adamant that she didn't want him visiting her and the baby while he was in such a state. However, he had other plans and strode up and down the corridor, opening the doors to different labour rooms and slamming them shut again when he found his girlfriend wasn't in them.

'I know she's in here!' he kept shouting. I called security who tried to persuade the man to leave quietly. His response was to take his shirt off in the middle of the corridor, and start wrestling with the porter. Security threw him out, much to our relief. In the mood he was in, he would have taken a swing at anyone.

Southampton is a large maternity unit and we have regional neo-natal, fetal and maternal services. This means that we often see women with a variety of existing medical conditions, as well as conditions relating to pregnancy. We also have babies that are known to have likely problems at birth. This often presents staff – both midwifery and obstetric – with complex care issues. We aim to be prepared in order for the women and their families to have the best experience they can. This is in addition to routine complications that can occur in pregnancy.

Sometimes women come in in strong labour with their baby in the breech position. These days most breeches are delivered by Caesarean, although if it's not a first baby and the baby's bottom is already hanging out we deliver it vaginally. The problem is not knowing exactly how the head is going to come out and we're always prepared for a quick dash to theatre if necessary.

If a woman comes in bleeding heavily before the baby has been born it may mean that the placenta has abrupted or broken away – a condition that can be life threatening for the mother and the baby. If the mother is bleeding heavily, the priority is to resuscitate and stabilise her, give her a blood transfusion if necessary and then assess the baby. It can be very difficult to prioritise in this way when two lives are at stake, but that is the order we have to do things in.

We are having more and more women coming into the unit with major cardiac problems. Previously they didn't survive childhood or were advised not to have children, but advances in medical care mean that they are able to have children, although they need a lot of care. When a woman with a heart condition is in labour very close monitoring is required and we have to be particularly careful about monitoring her fluid so as not to overload her heart.

Women who have type-1 diabetes are induced at thirty-eight weeks because there's an increased risk to the baby's well-being at the end of pregnancy. Women with existing diabetes are closely monitored when they are pregnant as is their baby 'on board'.

Some women have their diabetes controlled by diet prior to pregnancy, but as a result of their pregnancy and their increasing weight they may need to have insulin. The role of the midwife can then become one of an educator as well as a support. Mums need help in coming to terms with having to monitor their blood glucose more closely and administer their own insulin by injection. Diet advice is also very important, with a healthy, nutritional intake and regular meals being a priority. Sometimes we need to involve a dietician so that women get the most appropriate advice and encouragement to change bad habits.

Diabetes is a condition peculiar to pregnancy and women can develop what is know as gestational diabetes. Women from Africa and the Indian subcontinent are particularly prone, and so are all tested at twenty-eight weeks. Women who are overweight or who have a family history are also tested.

Women with diabetes usually have larger-than-average babies, and this is something that the midwife will be considering if she is caring for a diabetic mum in labour.

5

THE GREAT MELTING POT

It's very simple: what the lady says, goes. We will never ever perform an intervention without the woman's consent. Ever. What the lady says goes. However, you can say, 'I would recommend this'... and I have had women who have told me where to put my recommendations!

Dominique, episode 3

MARIA

Southampton is a rich melting pot of people from many different countries, religions and cultures. We now have a large Polish community, many of whom work at the docks, so we've been looking after a lot more Polish mums-to-be. We also look after a lot of women from Asian and African countries and if they don't speak much or any English this can cause problems during labour. Some women have been brought over here as brides and don't speak any English at all. Sometimes husbands and partners want to act as translators, but we really try to discourage that. They might not translate accurately, either because their own English isn't very good or because they don't want the midwife to know exactly what the woman is saying, or their wife to know exactly what the midwife is saying! Sometimes the woman's older children do the translation, which can be equally as complicated.

We produce information leaflets in many different languages about a variety of topics – they are useful, but no substitute for a proper conversation, especially if a problem suddenly arises. If we want to carry out a procedure for which we need consent, we have to make sure the woman understands what she's consenting to and that can be quite a challenge. Our only way of overcoming the language barrier is to make use of our interpreting service, and as much as we can we try to make sure the woman always sees the same interpreter so that she builds confidence in asking questions.

One of our midwives had to deal with a particularly difficult situation where the language barrier made things much harder. All midwives' worst nightmare is when we examine a pregnant woman and can't find a fetal heartbeat. One day a religious Muslim woman, clad in a burkha, arrived on labour ward with her husband. She was very young and spoke no English, but she seemed excited about the imminent birth. We discovered that she'd been brought over to the UK for an arranged marriage and had fallen pregnant soon after her wedding.

The midwife looking after her couldn't find a heartbeat and when it was confirmed that the baby had in fact died in her womb, this terrible news had to be communicated to her through her husband, because we didn't have a translator available. Her husband showed no sympathy or concern for her when he explained what had happened. He seemed to treat her like a second-class citizen.

'Oh, you made the baby die,' he said to her, accusingly.

The obstetric registrar tried to talk to the woman but her husband kept butting in. When an interpreter did arrive, he wasn't happy about it and we had to rely on a member of staff to provide a rough translation because he didn't object to that quite so much.

The woman then had to go through labour to have her baby, and it was distressing to see how she struggled to keep her body as covered up as possible throughout. We suggested that she might want to hold the baby after she had given birth to it, as mothers in this position often want or need to hold their baby and say goodbye to it.

Her husband objected strongly. 'She doesn't need to see the baby, in our culture we don't look at these babies,' he said. Then he decided that *he* would have a look at the baby, but wouldn't even tell his wife whether she'd given birth to a girl or a boy. The young woman wasn't allowed the opportunity even to see the baby she had carried.

Of course, the birth was distressing for all involved in her care. We try to respect everyone's cultural and religious traditions, but felt that he was incredibly unkind to his shocked, bewildered wife. The midwife who looked after the woman is from a similar background herself, and did not feel that this attitude was linked to any particular religious rules.

Midwives witness some beautiful deliveries involving families from different cultures. In one birth there were three generations of women in the room, all completely focused on looking after the woman who was in labour, encouraging and supporting her, massaging her body and feeding her sips of water – her grandmother, her mother and her sister.

After the baby was born, the grandmother picked it up and spoke to it very softly in the dimly lit room, introducing the new baby to the world and its new family. It was a very loving and moving thing to watch.

In some cultures we find that there are only muted celebrations when a woman gives birth to a girl. We've had mothers who turn their heads away when they give birth to a third female child. They are blamed for producing a baby of the 'wrong' sex. I've seen limousines arrive at the hospital to collect a woman who has given birth to a boy –

there's great pomp and ceremony, with drums and dancing. But when a girl is born, there are no such celebrations.

It can be hard to understand traditions that are unfamiliar to us, but it's not our place to judge and we always try to appreciate why things might be done in a different way. Some foreign-born women don't attend ante-natal clinics, for example, but then they might have come from a country where you're more likely to die if you go to hospital than if you don't. Some see a disfigurement as a curse on their family, rather than as a medical condition, and we have to explain to them how these things can arise and that they haven't been singled out in any way.

In some communities there is pressure on women not to have any pain relief during labour. One woman who was accompanied by her mother and mother-in-law. She had an epidural but didn't want them to know, so the midwife looking after her had to whisper to her when she was having a contraction so that she could fake the appropriate howling noises!

We look after some women from overseas who are asylum seekers or refugees. Nowadays in the NHS we all have to be mindful of how money is spent and ensure we make the best use of our resources. There is an expectation that midwives ask women their immigration status and for evidence that they have lived in the UK for a year or more. We really find this to be in conflict with our statutory responsibility to deliver clinical care. Culture, religion, background, disability or immigration status should not have any impact on the care we provide.

Poverty is a major issue for some of our mums. We have community midwives who do home visits and assess the housing situation for mothers-to-be. Sometimes they find families who are all living together in one room, with no cooking facilities. If we're dealing with families known to social services, we're often more aware of what the problems are, but there are more insidious cases where problems such as domestic violence are deliberately concealed, so that to the outside world everything appears fine. As midwives we often rely on our sixth sense in these situations. Sometimes body language or minor injuries can give the game away, or something the woman says or the way that she behaves doesn't quite add up.

Some women can be a product of their upbringing, and traumatic events in their past such as abuse can make them behave in a certain way. We do come across cases where women have been physically, sexually or emotionally abused in the past. Childhood sexual abuse is something we're rarely aware of as midwives, even though we know it's a problem that affects many women. Some women can be reluctant to have a vaginal examination when they're in labour because it makes them feel as if they're being violated once again. This was the case with one woman we looked after. It emerged after she'd given birth that she had been abused during her childhood by several male members of her family. We know that this sort of abuse happens and I believe midwives should be given more training to deal with these problems. Women who have been abused are particularly vulnerable during pregnancy and childbirth. Those bodily fluids and the brutality of something coming through your body can be difficult for the woman to bear.

Women often struggle valiantly to do the best for their child in social circumstances that are very difficult. We hear about the terrible cases like that of Baby Peter, but we don't hear enough about all the cases where mothers are up against extraordinary odds to love, care for and protect their children and somehow manage to do so. Unbelievably in the twenty-first century, in a wealthy country like ours, we still have cases where a mother goes hungry in order to feed her children. Some women face extraordinary odds and they receive no acknowledgement.

Some couples arrive at the hospital and we get the feeling as the woman's labour progresses that their relationship isn't going to last. Other couples are very lovey dovey, and we assume it will be a case of 'till death do us part'. But sometimes you hear later that the lovebirds have split and the ones whose relationship looked rocky have stayed the course. Labour isn't always the most accurate time to make an assessment about the health of a relationship!

All kinds of relationship issues can become evident when a woman goes into labour. We had one case where a woman had been having relationships with two men simultaneously – one was black and the other was white. The baby was born black, which confirmed to her who the father was. Quite how she broke the news to the other man in her life, I'm not sure, but I certainly wouldn't have wanted to be in her shoes.

In another case, a man arrived on labour ward with his partner. He looked very familiar to one of the midwives but she couldn't quite place him. 'Where do I recognise you from?' she kept saying. He shrugged and replied that he didn't recognise her at all. When she left the room he followed her out and whispered, 'I'll tell you why you recognise me. I was here two weeks ago with my wife, and now I'm here with my girlfriend. Neither knows about the other. Whatever you do, *please* don't say anything,' he implored her.

'Of course I won't say anything,' she replied, although I'm sure she had her own opinions about his behaviour. As midwives it's not our job to judge anyone, but situations like that where you know that a man is deceiving two women who have just given birth makes you feel quite morally queasy.

Some homes we visit are desperately poor and insanitary – it can be very difficult to suggest that the environment is a less than ideal one to bring a new baby into. One woman had birds flying around her home, and bird droppings everywhere.

'How are you going to manage your home when the baby comes?' I asked her, trying to sound tactful but imagining the absolute chaos of trying to look after a new baby in the middle of this aviary. It's not easy having those conversations, and you have to accept that some people choose to live in a certain way that might not be what we'd like for ourselves. Some people have lots of cats and we explain that they mustn't be allowed to prowl across work surfaces. If I felt that an environment was unsafe, I would report it to social services straight away. At one tiny flat that I visited, I had a rather close encounter with a huge Newfoundland dog that pinned me against the wall. Apart from being quite terrifying, it seemed to take up every available inch of space in the flat.

'And where are you going to put the baby ...?' I asked, nervously.

There are women we deal with who are living in such bad conditions that they aren't able to maintain basic personal hygiene. Occasionally we have women whose pubic hair is crawling with lice. You just have to do your best to avoid these tiny creatures and get on with the task in hand.

Some people start babies off in a drawer, rather than a cot which is fine because, despite all the fancy stuff that's available these days, babies need very little to start off with. Travellers wouldn't dream of doing that though. They say that every new baby has to have a new cot and a whole new wardrobe of clothes.

Southampton has a significant traveller community and when I was a senior midwifery manager we set up a little team to support pregnant travellers. Whenever a travelling community comes through Southampton, the council phones us to tell us if there's a pregnant woman amongst them. Travellers don't have a particularly good track record when it comes to accessing healthcare, but we've built up good and trusting relationships and many of the women do keep coming back to us each time they get pregnant. We have a particularly good relationship with the travellers who are based on the permanent site on the east side of the city.

I looked after one of these women – a very quiet and gentle young girl. She'd attended all her ante-natal appointments and her baby appeared to be developing well. She went into labour spontaneously and nothing untoward appeared to be happening, but as the labour became more intense the baby's heartbeat suddenly stopped. It seemed that the baby had died in the womb, for no obvious reason at all. Sadly she gave birth to a stillborn baby. As soon as the news spread through the travellers' community, many people wanted to come not only from Southampton, but also from surrounding areas to pay their respects.

Because of our relationship with the travellers and the local authority, the latter turned a blind eye to the many travellers who descended on the area. The immediate family of around fifteen people wanted to see the baby and bless it. Then another thirty extended family members arrived in Southampton to come and pay their respects and temporarily moved onto the permanent travellers' site. I was happy that we were able to accommodate the influx without any problems, and touched by the support this young woman received.

The young woman came back to meet with me and her consultant obstetrician a few weeks after the stillbirth to discuss what had happened. The fact she agreed to come back showed real trust in us. It appeared that the cord had wrapped itself around the baby's neck, cutting off its oxygen supply – a sad occurrence that nobody could have done anything about.

It was hard not to feel that we'd let the woman down, even though the post-mortem showed that there was nothing that could have been done to prevent this situation from arising.

We offer a birth afterthought service where women can phone up and go through the notes of their labour with a professional if there's anything they'd like to discuss. If they're anxious about something that happened first time round, a plan is put in place to make sure it doesn't happen a second time. As midwives, we have a special relationship with the women we're looking after – generally we're looking after well women, so we start the relationship off on an equal footing. Often women ask for the same midwife they had for their first pregnancy for later pregnancies – you could describe it as a professional friendship. Even though there are times when the outcome might not be positive, it's still important to give of our best, to listen carefully to what the woman is saying and to work together with her. We all come to work wanting to do a good job and have a sense of pride in providing the best possible care.

We visited the travellers' site several times in the year after the stillbirth and the woman and her family always came out of their caravan to say hello to us. When the young woman got pregnant again she came back to us, which I felt showed an enormous amount of trust. By the time she came back the second time, we'd worked through what had happened the first time and she had grown to accept it.

Travellers are extremely loving towards their children and show them a huge amount of respect. They lavish large sums on preparations for a new baby and insist on having the best of everything. Happily, everything was absolutely fine with this young woman's second baby. Understandably she and her husband were extremely anxious throughout the labour and it was so lovely to be able to hand her a perfect baby.

ROS

Some religions recite a prayer soon after the baby is born. It's really lovely to see a father cradling his baby, whispering secrets of life into its ear and praying. Sometimes a religious leader arrives at the hospital after a birth and says prayers to mark the arrival of a new life.

When very devout Muslim women arrive on labour ward we have to negotiate with them about how much of their clothing they're prepared to take off. When there are issues, it's difficult to know if not removing her clothing is what the woman wants or what her husband wants. Some women insist on keeping their head and body covered for as long as possible during labour. It can be very alien for them to have their body exposed in any way so we try to do our examinations under a sheet and do our utmost to protect their modesty and respect their wishes.

But although different women have different approaches to how much of their bodies they are prepared to expose during labour, the process of birth itself is a great leveller. Whether women are rich or poor, or follow one religion or another, every woman is undergoing a broadly similar experience.

Women who are religious do bring their faith into the labour room. Some bring bibles or copies of the Koran or religious music. I remember praying when I was pushing my son Duncan out. To some people, faith is a great support and comfort. People who believe in astrology look at their stars to try to work out what kind of a birth they'll have.

A lot of people ask me, 'What time is the baby going to be born?' as if I have some sort of mystical abilities which allow me to see into the future. Nobody can predict something like that accurately − if I could I'd be a very rich woman! If it's 2 a.m. when I'm asked that question, I try to sidestep it by replying, 'It will be born today'.

Labour can be a very unpredictable business and no one can gaze into a crystal ball and know whether it is going to suddenly speed up or slow down. Right up to the last minute, things can change. One of the things I love about the job is this unpredictability. Thankfully, we're not working on a production line in a baked beans factory. Even if I'm looking after two women who have similarly straightforward labours, the two births will be very different because of the different personalities involved and the way they react to their situation.

We see some very interesting tattoos and piercings in our line of work. I've seen women who have had their clitoris pierced and although it's not directly in the line of fire, it can cause problems if the woman tears. Something to think about if you're fond of unusual piercings! People think of the vagina tearing backwards during birth, but it can also tear forwards and a pierced clitoris could make that situation worse. If a woman ends up having to go down to theatre, all jewellery must be removed including tongue studs and nose rings. I usually suggest that women remove all their jewellery right away, as there might not be time to do it later on if an emergency arises and the woman is rushed down to theatre. It's also important that a woman isn't wearing nail varnish because if problems arise, looking at the colour of her nail bed can be a good indication of her state of health at that moment. Sometimes I get a sense that a woman might end up in theatre and in those cases I'm particularly keen to get all adornments removed as soon as possible.

Older children sometimes end up in the room when their mother is in labour because there is nowhere else for them to go. I notice that the children often look quite scared, and I wonder what effect it has on them to see their mother screaming and in pain. Some of them might find it hard to get their head round the fact that they also came into the world that way, and caused their mum a lot of pain in the process. A child's mother is the most important person in their life and if you see them looking vulnerable, bleeding or rushed off to theatre, it can undermine their sense of security and can be terrifying for them even if everything's explained afterwards. If older children do end up on labour ward, we've occasionally had to set up a temporary family room for them. We try really hard to be family friendly, but it's very hard to have children running up and down and we just don't have the staff to look after them.

If a woman has planned to have a home birth and decides right from the start that she wants her children there, she can prepare them throughout the pregnancy and let them decide whether or not they want to attend the birth. If they'd rather not be there, they can simply go off and play in their bedroom or watch television. But in a rushed, emergency situation in a hospital there is little opportunity to prepare older siblings.

A woman is more likely to turn up at the hospital with her older children if she goes into labour in the middle of the night, or if she's newly arrived in the UK and doesn't have a network of family and friends that she can rely on. Very occasionally older children who accompany their mother to hospital when she goes into labour might be put into temporary foster care if there's no one else to look after them.

I looked after a woman who arrived in labour accompanied by her sister, not her husband. She was in some distress and explained that she'd been raped and wasn't sure if the baby was her husband's or the rapist's. She was absolutely desperate to keep the whole thing from her husband – it was terribly sad. The rapist was Asian, so she thought she would know immediately who was the father of the baby. If it wasn't her husband's, then she would have the baby adopted and would tell her husband that it had died. Unfortunately, the baby was born with dark hair but fairly pale skin. Lots of mixed-race babies are born with very light skin that goes darker over time. So she didn't get the definite answer she wanted. We never got to find out what decision she made after the birth, but cases like hers remind us that birth isn't a straightforward, joyous event for every woman.

Popular culture has an influence on the names that people give to their babies. I remember one woman decided to name her baby after Pamela Anderson's character on *Baywatch*, CJ. Many of us had never watched *Baywatch* so we had no clue who CJ was! Soap characters are an inspiration for some parents and obviously these names have changed over the decades. We used to have a few Sue Ellens when *Dallas* was on, now *EastEnders* and *Coronation Street* are big influences, or the names celebrities choose for their children. Some parents choose names from nature like Sky, River, Tree and Willow. We always try and be enthusiastic about parents' choices, no matter what we might think about the names they pick! One couple had twins and called one baby John Robert and the other one Robert John! I think the most unusual name I've ever come across was Dwayne Pipe – first name Dwayne, second name Pipe. To this day I'm not sure if the parents were aware of what they'd inflicted on their child!

Sometimes couples can't agree on a name. This research isn't remotely scientific, but we've noticed that sometimes if a woman asserts her wish for a particular name *after* the baby has been born but *before* the placenta has been delivered, the man will cave in and let her have her own way. Take note ladies!

When women come into the hospital in labour they bring all kinds of people with them – not only their partners, but sometimes their mothers, fathers, mothers-in-law and assorted friends, too. We often have relatives phoning up, but we need to be careful about confidentiality on the phone. A wife might be phoning up about her husband's lover, you just never know! So we only give information to the next of kin and try to be as diplomatic as possible. Sometimes a woman's mother might phone for an update, but it might not be a convenient moment for the daughter to get to the phone, or she might not want to speak to her mother at all. In those instances you have to tactfully suggest that her partner calls back at a convenient moment.

Strange phone calls are part of life on the maternity ward. One woman called the other day and said she wanted to find out how her boyfriend's sister's getting on but she said she couldn't remember her name. Very odd!

When a woman arrives in labour, the whole universe revolves around her. We have seventeen rooms, all occupied at some point by women who have emptied their minds of all thoughts apart from the task in hand. During the summer we have the windows open and the disembodied wailing of a woman in labour in a room down the corridor might drift into the room where I'm looking after another woman. She's unlikely to have ever met the woman making all the noise, but when she senses that the other woman is about to deliver I'll often notice the woman holding her breath, waiting to hear the sound of the baby crying. If you walk into the labour ward when it's at its busiest, it often looks deserted because all the activity is going on behind closed doors in the labour rooms – it's the opposite of what you'd expect a busy place to look like.

Women from different backgrounds and cultures have their own ways of dealing with pain – some are very quiet and stoical, while others are very vocal. Some women only want their partner there, while others bring their whole extended family or sometimes what feels like the whole neighbourhood. The delivery rooms aren't too big – generally there's only room for two other people, so there can be conflict about who's going to stay with the woman and who's going to wait outside until after the baby is born. Once the woman's had the baby, all the friends and relatives who've been pacing up and down the corridor want to go straight in. It amazes me how many people do turn up in the middle of the night – aunties, brothers, cousins – quite happy to be on standby for hours on end until the baby is born. We try to say that just two people are allowed into the room at a time, but keeping excited relatives under control can be as difficult as stopping the tide coming in. When I told one relative firmly that the woman who had just given birth couldn't have any more visitors she begged and pleaded with me to let her into the delivery room.

'Oh, please can I just have a peek at the baby?' she said. 'I've come a long way.' I relented, thinking that maybe she'd come from somewhere like Manchester. It turned out she'd come from about two miles down the road!

6

STRANGE GOINGS ON

When all the rooms are full it can be quite eerie. The noise kind of floats across in the night ... this sort of disembodied voice, screaming; it can be quite unnerving. When I come on at night and there are women wandering the corridors, I wonder if they're walking up and down thinking, When is it going to be my turn?

Ros, episode 4

MARIA

In labour, pretty much anything goes and as midwives we really do see it all. We're looking after a much wider range of women than ever before – women from different cultures, older women, younger women, women who previously would never have been able to have children because of pre-existing medical conditions such as congenital heart defects and cystic fibrosis.

Lots of women make birth plans, but we often find that women who are pregnant with their first child have expectations of how their labour and birth will be, and then they find the reality is actually quite different. We often have women arriving on labour ward with a detailed birth plan stipulating that even if the going gets tough, they should be given no pain relief because they are determined to have a completely 'natural' birth. I must admit that I chuckle to myself when I see these, because often these are the women who end up having every intervention that modern science can offer.

My heart sinks when a woman hands us a plan the length of a dissertation – even if there's sensible material in there, like keeping mobile during labour and putting the baby on the woman's tummy immediately after birth. We think it's more important to be aware of how long the labour is likely to take and how women are likely to cope with the pain, rather than stipulating what sort of 'extras' they would like. In the construction of birth plans, the most important thing is to have a healthy baby; how you get there is secondary.

We advise mums-to-be not to be too proscriptive with their birth plans, because labour can be a very unpredictable business and no woman knows exactly how she'll deal with the experience before it happens. I would prefer to call the birth plan a 'wish list' for labour. Sometimes couples will have drawn up a spider diagram – if *this*

93

happens I'll do *this*, if *that* happens I'll do *that* and so on. These plans can be really helpful in supporting the decision that needs to be made if things don't quite go to plan. These flexible, realistic plans can enhance the sense of achievement everyone feels at the end.

Many midwives will tell you how teachers hold a special place in their heart – more than any other profession, they have a reputation for having high expectations of their birth experience. They often expect extremely – and sometimes impossibly – high standards of themselves.

Women bring all kinds of things with them when they arrive at the hospital in labour. We often tell them to bring their own pillow because we never seem to have enough of them. Everyone remembers poor Joy, who carried her own pillows up and down the hospital corridors whilst she was waiting and waiting for her labour to progress. Some women don't stop with pillows, though, and bring half the household with them – including enough food to feed a small army. I wonder how long some of them are planning to stay when they come so laden down! Some of the younger mums bring their favourite teddy with them, which really highlights their youth and is always touching to see.

Alternative therapies are increasingly popular, and a lot of women are keen to try out new ways of alleviating pain or creating a calming atmosphere. One of our midwives is a trained reflexologist and, where appropriate, offers this service to the women she's looking after, sometimes with amazing results. A few years ago there was a woman who was really struggling and rolling around on the bed in pain, so one of the staff went out of the room to get her some pethidine. But while she was gone, the midwife performed reflexology on the woman's feet and she returned with the drugs to find the woman had fallen into a peaceful sleep. Of course, we would only use this kind of alternative therapy if the midwife had received appropriate training in it.

Hypno-birthing classes are popular with some women. These teach women self-hypnosis and specialised breathing techniques to help them get through labour. Some women like to have a lavender fragrance in the room to soothe them, or they drink camomile tea. We wouldn't dismiss any calming things like that that the women have faith in.

A mum that I looked after who was having a planned Caesarean particularly wanted as calm an environment as possible and requested soft lights and music in the operating theatre. We agreed to her request and the atmosphere was really lovely. The baby was delivered and put straight onto her chest and it didn't feel as if we were in an operating theatre at all.

Women who don't realise they're pregnant until they go in to labour are more common than many people realise. I can think of three cases where babies were born down the toilet at home, to women and girls who had no idea they were pregnant. The first we usually hear about it is when we get a panicked phone call.

We had one situation where a girl of thirteen had concealed a pregnancy until it was too late for a termination to be a possible option. She said she'd been forced to have sex with a boy not much older than her, and was understandably quite traumatised. She and the family wanted a Caesarean section followed by adoption, and she'd decided she wasn't going to hold the baby after the birth. In the end, though, she changed her mind, cuddled her baby and gave it a name. It was incredibly sad and moving to watch. Whatever the circumstances leading to a pregnancy, there is a powerful bond between a mother and the baby she has carried inside her for nine months.

The consequences of concealed pregnancies are sometimes very sad. The earlier support is accessed, the better the outcome tends to be.

There are other times when a birth is not as joyful as it should be. One of my colleagues, Eileen, told me about delivering a baby for a woman whose husband had died when she was pregnant. When she was in labour, Eileen really felt as if there was an extra presence in the room. It was very hard for her to describe. When the baby was born, the woman cuddled it, silently. After fifteen minutes she spoke.

'Paul was with us. He never left my side for the whole of the labour and now that he's seen his baby safely born, he's gone,' she said, calmly.

It was very emotional, but at the same time Eileen said there was a great feeling of peace in the room after the baby was born.

Eileen also looked after a woman whose first baby had died at the age of six months from a cardiac condition. She was understandably anxious about the birth of her second baby, and very emotional. Happily, the baby was born without complication and everything was fine, but when the new baby took its first breath, Eileen felt a shiver run down her spine. She said she felt a strong sense of the first baby's spirit in the room. It wasn't anything she could see, hear, touch or explain, but there was an extra presence in that room at that moment. I believe that sometimes the spirits of the living and the dead can collide at the moment of birth.

Whatever it was that Eileen felt in the room at that moment, it seemed the mother felt it too. There was a powerful, unspoken bond between the mother and the midwife, a kind of silent recognition that there was someone or something else in the room at the moment of the second baby's birth.

ROS

Like all professions we midwives have our own shorthand.
When a woman's labour is progressing well we say she's
really 'cracking on'. When a woman has had her baby we
write 'del' to show that the baby's been delivered. A few
years ago we had a manager who wanted to make some
changes to the way we worked. She told us that babies were
born and pizzas were delivered, but we just couldn't get used
to the change. One of the most important sayings we use
here on the labour ward is, 'Mrs Brown is fully . . .' or 'Mrs
Brown is on the phone . . .' This means that there's a nice
pot of freshly made tea in the office! We use 'multips' to
refer to women who have had several pregnancies. We have
a saying, 'Never trust a multip', because one minute they
might appear to be in the early stages of labour and the next
minute the baby's head is coming out.

We use 'FI' or 'MI' to denote a female or male infant.
Sometimes when medical students come onto the ward
they panic when they see the initials MI, because in general
medical terms an MI is a cardiac incident. We've often had
alarmed students asking if a woman has had an MI – meaning a heart attack. The midwife has to explain that she's just
given birth to a boy.

We do sometimes use the abbreviation 'FLK', meaning
'funny looking kid', although obviously not in front of the
parents! 'VE' is a vaginal examination, not a significant event

in the Second World War. A 'BBA' is a baby 'born before arrival' at the hospital.

Some women have very unusual demands in labour. There was one woman who insisted on watching *Coronation Street* right through her labour. For many women childbirth is a time where they want peace and quiet and retreat into their primal selves. It's probably a little bit harder to attain that state when you're avidly following the fortunes of your favourite soap stars in between contractions. We did suggest turning the television off, but she refused. Apparently there was a significant wedding taking place in that particular episode and she didn't want to miss it. The baby was born mid-way through the ceremony!

Women in labour can be very superstitious. They don't like the thought of giving birth on Friday the thirteenth and we don't have a delivery room thirteen.

Some women have no apparent contractions at all. We had a very unusual case recently of a young woman who arrived on labour ward saying she thought her waters might have broken. She complained of some backache but nothing more and didn't appear to be in much pain or discomfort. When I examined her I could feel that she was having contractions, which seemed to be the cause of her backache. But she just couldn't feel them at all. I put her on the monitor and said I would get one of the doctors to come and see her in a little while. I thought that things were at a very early stage because she wasn't even in pain yet, so

I went off to look after some of the other women and put a student midwife in charge of monitoring her. A little while later, to my amazement, the student came and told me that she was fully dilated.

'How on earth did that happen so quickly?' I asked.

I went to examine her and could see that the baby's head was very low and that it was time for her to push. But she was still not getting any contractions, and apart from her slight backache felt absolutely fine! I asked her to push when she got backache but that was only happening about once every ten minutes. The doctor agreed she needed a hormone drip to strengthen the contractions. This was given to her and she delivered a healthy baby soon afterwards, yet still hadn't felt a single contraction. It's amazing how different women's bodies can be. I don't know what it was about that woman's body that enabled her to give birth without painful contractions but whatever it was, I'm sure she was the envy of every other woman on labour ward that night!

Occasionally we get hoax calls on labour ward. One night I answered the ward phone and got a bizarre message in a weird electronic voice. The message said, 'I'm in a lot of pain, can you tell my friend?' The phone rang again later with another electronic-voice text message saying, 'This is getting really painful, can you ring my friend's number?'

I rang both the number the message had come from and the friend's number, but got no reply from either. Then we received another message saying, 'In a lot of pain and really frightened'. I phoned the number again and this time a woman answered and said she was having contractions. I phoned the friend again and this time her mother answered and said the girl was out for the evening. I asked where and she said in Manchester. It all sounded very odd, and I asked the woman if she knew about her daughter's friend being pregnant and in labour and she sounded very vague about the whole thing. Next I phoned the girl who was in labour again and said, 'Your friend isn't available. You really need to come into the hospital. We'll send someone round to come and bring you in.'

The girl sounded panicked. 'My dad is out and he doesn't know I'm pregnant. If he comes home and finds an ambulance here for me because I'm having a baby hc'll be really violent.'

I eventually managed to persuade her to let me send one of the midwives round to check her over. She gave me an address not far from the hospital, so I phoned one of the midwives on call and she agreed to go round there, while I kept her talking on the phone. When the on-call midwife arrive at the address, an old lady came to the door and looked completely blank.

'There's no girl here having a baby,' she said.

'You gave the wrong address, didn't you?' I said. After a pause she replied, 'The baby has just been born.'

'Is the baby crying? Do you have a towel? Can you wrap it up?' the midwife asked, feeling really concerned that a girl who we knew nothing about had apparently just given birth completely alone. The girl became very vague again, continued to refuse to give me her proper address and then hung up. I tried redialling but couldn't get hold of her again.

We filled in an incident form and someone tracked her down a few days later. It turned out that she wasn't pregnant at all. There were times during the phone call when I was *sure* there was something not right, especially when she gave the wrong address, but she had sounded genuinely distressed and in pain on the phone. We have to treat these cases as genuine unless or until proved otherwise, because when we don't have the full facts we can't afford to let a woman who might genuinely be in labour slip through the net.

A few months ago I got an email from another hospital saying there was a similar incident somewhere else, and I wonder if it was the same girl trying to fool another labour ward.

We dealt with another case with some similarities to that one. A young girl turned up at the desk looking terribly anxious. She explained that she was pregnant and had lost a baby before. She just wanted some reassurance that the baby's heart was still beating. She arrived without the handheld notes that pregnant women usually carry around with them. She was quite plump and said she was about twenty weeks pregnant or a bit less. I checked on the computer and there was no record of her name being booked in, which is what women generally do as soon as their pregnancy is confirmed. Concerned, I went to speak to the gynaecologist about her.

'Do a scan,' she said. 'I bet she's not pregnant.' So that's what I did, and sure enough, there was no baby.

'We've done the scan and it seems that you're not actually pregnant,' I said. She didn't react at all and simply walked off. It may be that she genuinely thought she was pregnant – the desire for a baby can do funny things to a woman's mind and emotions – or she could just have been deliberately wasting our time.

Although sex is a crucial precursor to getting pregnant, we don't expect it to actually happen on the labour ward. But on a couple of occasions midwives have caught women and their partners in the act. On one occasion a midwife noticed that the curtains were pulled tightly shut around one of the beds on the post-natal ward. She could hear some suspicious rustling behind the curtain, tentatively pulled it back and to her amazement caught a couple having very energetic sex! Needless to say, sex is not permitted on the wards and we don't advise women to resume sexual activity until after their six-week check-up for health reasons. Apparently they were quite put out about the interruption!

7

DADS AND OTHER
BIRTH PARTNERS

It is really difficult for men, because when women come into the hospital and they're in pain, a lot of the midwives' attention is focused on making sure we're getting all of her wishes and needs met. And then sometimes you have a look and there's this guy in the corner not quite knowing what to do, what to say, how to act.

Michelle, episode 6

ROS

Encouraging dads to be in the delivery room is something that happened as part of a much bigger shift in attitudes towards childbirth which began in the 1970s. In the past giving birth was all about doing what the doctors told you, but now we try to make it much more inclusive for everyone – including the midwives! In some countries, the midwives look after the women in labour and then a doctor delivers the baby. That seems very unfair on the midwives, who do all the hard work, encouraging the woman through a long and often exhausting labour, only for the doctor to walk in at the last moment and triumphantly deliver the baby – a bit like a magician pulling a rabbit out of a hat.

It has taken some of the medical professionals a bit of time to adjust to the idea that women and their partners could be involved in the decision-making process. There was one midwife who has retired now who was a classic Yorkshire woman – she always called a spade a spade. When a couple arrived on the labour ward she used to say, 'Now, daddy, you stay over there quietly in the corner. Mummy and I are going to have a baby.' She had quite a sharp tongue and I'm sure she would have preferred it if the men had kept out of the delivery room altogether. But she tolerated them as long as they kept quiet, behaved and didn't inter-fere. Once she'd issued her stern instructions to them, they all sat there like meek little lambs, terrified of moving in case she chastised them.

As the years have passed, men have been allowed out of the chair in the corner and have graduated to standing next to the bed. Labour units are far more relaxed now about the role of the dads – we like to chat to the dads about their jobs and whether or not this is their first baby to make them feel relaxed too. It's surprising how many men are squeamish and go out of the room if their partner has to have blood taken. And that's before they've seen anything of the blood and gore of the birth!

We remind the men that they need to eat and drink to keep their strength up. Although they're obviously not going through what the woman is going through, it can be a gruelling marathon, even as a spectator sport. If they haven't bothered to eat and drink they're more likely to keel over at a critical moment. We tell them that if they start to feel funny they need to sit down or leave the room because if they fall and bang their heads they'll have to go to A&E and might miss the birth.

I remember one woman who was having her third baby. She was a calm, sensible woman with a tall, skinny, gangly husband. The baby was about to be delivered and its heartbeat had dropped a bit, which isn't unusual just before delivery. The baby was a bit pale and floppy when it was born and a brisk rub with a towel wasn't enough to get things going. It needed to be taken outside for some oxygen.

'Don't worry, the baby is going to be fine,' I said. Someone took the baby outside to administer some oxygen and at that moment the woman's husband collapsed into a nearby chair. His wife had only just given birth, but she was much more calm and controlled than he was. She sat on the edge of the bed and calmly tried to coax him back to consciousness.

'Don't worry. He's always like that,' she said in a matter-of-fact tone, obviously used by now to his sensitive constitution.

A lot of dads are technologically minded and love machines. If I put the monitor on, I always explain what the different hieroglyphics mean so that they feel included in the action. We find that a lot of men ask questions all the time which can be quite exhausting for the midwife – they've read all the baby books, trawled the most obscure corners of the internet and arrive thinking they know everything . . . even though they often don't.

I looked after one woman who screamed and screamed as her labour progressed. She was accompanied by her very slightly-built husband. As her pain intensified, she gripped him more and more tightly, grabbing him by his clothing. Each time she grabbed him, she ripped a bit more of his shirt off. By the time the baby was born the poor man was standing there with little more than his underpants intact. He took the whole thing in his stride though.

'I've put this baby here so now I'm going to take the consequences like a man,' he said, grinning sheepishly.

All births are different, but one thing that's *always* the same is the moment the dad has to get the vest, nappy and babygro out of the bag the woman has brought with her. At this point the men are, without exception, useless. The poor woman has gone to so much trouble to pack the bag neatly full of lovely, new baby clothes, and then the men cause havoc by rummaging around in the bag and pulling out anything they can find. Then, completely baffled, they hold up various tiny garments and ask, 'What's a vest? Is this a nappy?'

Joy's husband, Fabio, severely tested her patience when, having finally made the decision to undergo a Caesarean after several days of labour, he was unable to locate the right items of clothing in the bag she'd packed. Poor Fabio!

Some partners adopt the role of cheerleaders and put their all into encouraging the woman to push. Others are at a complete loss about what to do and stand there helpless and bewildered, sometimes attracting anger from their women because they're being so useless. It's sometimes hard not to feel sorry for the men though, especially if it's their first baby, because the whole experience is a complete foreign country to them and they're witnessing the woman they love behaving in a totally irrational way, the like of which they've never seen before. And to make matters worse, they're being blamed for everything. There should definitely be some kind of reassuring guide available for new dads, explaining that just because their partner says terrible things to them in the throes of labour, it doesn't mean that they're heading for the divorce court as soon as the cord is cut.

When the woman has expressed strong ideas in the birth plan about what she does and doesn't want in labour, but then wants to deviate from the plan – for example by having an epidural when her birth plan stipulates no epidural under any circumstances – the man can be at a bit of a loss about what to do. Sometimes in those situations the midwife has to act as a go-between and try to negotiate a solution that will be acceptable to both. Or, he might end up making fun of her, like Steve, who memorably teased his poor wife Tracy for using pain relief when she'd said beforehand that she wouldn't. His behaviour in the delivery room was definitely a real talking point!

We do have men who insist on doing all the talking for their wives or partners. This often occurs if the woman doesn't speak good English, although sometimes the woman can speak more English than we realise and it's just that the man wants to be the one in control. Some men feel they're absolutely indispensable to the whole process and find it quite hard to accept that if they weren't there the woman would still have the baby!

Dads need to understand that a certain point comes in the labour when they need to stop cheering the woman on and let her just listen to one voice – the midwife issuing instructions about when to push and when not to push. There's a time when the woman needs to concentrate on breathing rather than pushing and if the man's shouting 'push, push!' it can be very disorientating.

If the dad is a doctor he might find it hard to stop behaving like a doctor when his partner is in labour. If the woman needs a canula inserting for a drip, the doctor dad sometimes leaps forward and says, 'I'll do that'.

'No you won't,' is always our firm response. 'You're not here as a doctor but as a dad. You have to leave your profession at the door of the labour room.'

They often want to know every little medical detail about what's going on, whereas I've found that if the woman giving birth is a doctor, she's generally happy to abdicate all medical responsibility and leave the job to the professionals who are looking after her.

I once looked after a couple who were both litigation solicitors. The husband was writing down everything that happened and everything anyone said. He asked the names of everyone who came into the room and wrote them down too. It was all very scary. I was so relieved when everything went well with the labour and the birth and we weren't saddled with a malpractice action after the birth.

We expect to have partners at births, but sometimes female friends, mothers or mothers-in-law come along as well or instead. I was very surprised when Tracy and Steve chose to have their eighteen-year-old son Liam present at the birth. Not too many mums are reproducing over a couple of decades these days. She must have a very close relationship with her son to have wanted him to be there . . . and for him to want to be there.

Many dads cry when the baby is born, which is entirely natural and very moving. The woman is absolutely exhausted at this point and joy, relief and exhaustion form a potent cocktail of emotions in the labour room. Men sometimes think that it's not manly to cry but that's non-sense. It's far better to show emotion than to conceal it and I love to see the men crying tears of joy.

MARIA

By the time I started to train as a midwife, it was already expected that fathers would want to be present at births, but it still wasn't assumed that they would automatically be there mopping the brow of the woman they love. The childbirth expert Michel Odent, who popularised the use of water births, believes that men in the delivery room are an obstacle rather than an asset to the process of labour and birth, but overwhelmingly now men are present at the birth of their children. The role of the father in the family has changed a lot – he's much more involved in childcare and most families have an expectation that the father will be fully involved in the child's life, and that includes being present at the birth.

Many men have never been exposed to what childbirth is all about and seeing the bloody, agonising reality can come as a total shock to them. We offer parent education classes and try to prepare men for seeing their partner in a great deal of pain and talk to them about how they might feel about that. Some men can be quite traumatised by their first experience of childbirth, because they couldn't do anything to take away the pain their loved one was in.

Men are often used to being able to fix things, but often struggle when they realise that labour is one situation that they can't 'problem solve'. Many find it hard to be totally reliant on a professional they have barely met, one who is assuring them that their partner thrashing around on the bed in the most terrible pain is perfectly normal. For men to be able to acknowledge that, beyond being present and offering supportive words of encouragement and a mopped brow, there is nothing useful they can do is hard. I have had men break down crying when their partner was rushed down to theatre for a Caesarean because they felt so helpless.

Men are never prepared for the amount of time birth takes. They're never prepared for babies that take an age to put in an appearance, nor for the ones which pop out unexpectedly quickly. They're never prepared for the amount of pain the woman experiences, nor for the way she changes in labour. The woman may not want the man to go near her and she may scream and shout in a way she never would in her normal life. Women often go into themselves when they're in labour and don't want to talk very much. The birth process changes the level of communication between the couple. Even when we're very poorly we communicate with our loved ones as our normal selves, but during that intense period before women give birth they retreat verbally and only communicate where necessary.

I say to partners, 'She may want you to stroke and hold her, or she may push you away. Be prepared for a whole spectrum of reactions. There's no telling how a woman will respond to the intensity of the experience of giving birth.' When women are in the throes of such terrible pain, they won't know what they want. They don't know what they can do to make it better, it's just something they have to go through and that's really hard. Sometimes they want to be with their mother rather than their partner, feeling that labour is something that only women can understand. However engaged the partner is, he's quite often excluded.

Although there are different theories about whether men should or shouldn't be present at the birth of their child, my view is that it would be a shame for partners to miss out on the emotional moment of birth.

Not all women choose to have a male partner at the birth, though. Some don't have a male partner and others choose somebody they feel will be the best support to them – mother, mother-in-law or a friend. Some women want more than one person to be with them. We try to encourage women to not have more than two people with them, because there's no space for more in the delivery rooms. There are times when having two birth partners is really beneficial, though – when one has run out of energy the other person who is less weary, can take over. If the birth is happening at home then of course there can be more people present – including their other children. Some people feel that children shouldn't be present when their mother is giving birth, but provided they're prepared properly for what they're going to witness, I think it can be okay. These mums have included their children in all other areas of their lives and they don't see why their kids should be excluded from this experience. The mother is centre stage and we respect whoever she chooses to have around her in childbirth. Of course, I would never undertake any kind of examination without checking whether or not the woman is happy for the other person or people in the room to witness it.

We hear a lot of criticism of teenage parents and suggestions that they're unable to be good parents. It was great to see Ross, the youngest dad in the series, being so supportive to his girlfriend Abbie, even telling her to bite his hand. He was more willing to share in that experience than some older men, and together with Abbie's mum they made a really supportive team. He seemed to know instinctively how best to support her, and it was tremendously moving to see their connection.

We all loved Penny Rainbow's husband, Ben. 'This is all about you and I'll do whatever you want me to do,' he said. If there's such a thing as an ideal dad in the delivery room, he'd be it! I think the series was quite representative of the range of fathers we see in the delivery rooms.

It's important for women and their partners to discuss,

long before the woman goes into labour, how they are both likely to feel and what's the best way for him to support her. However, although it's important to be prepared, nobody can predict exactly how they'll feel when they're actually going through the whole thing. Labour is not about a woman failing or succeeding; doing a good job or a bad job. Labour can be the difference between running a mile and a marathon. We try to explain labour to partners in these terms, as the whole thing can be very hard for men to get their heads round.

We see lots of dads burst into tears when the baby is born. They are just overcome by the intensity of the whole situation and are crying with complete relief and joy that the baby is out at last and healthy. I have had one dad faint on me. There's nothing you can do other than put their head on a pillow and wait for them to come round. Quite often it's not about the blood and gore of childbirth, but about the intensity of the experience and the warmth of the room. One husband who was from an army background demonstrated a stiff upper lip throughout his wife's labour. She had had an epidural and was so exhausted she kept nodding off. He kept slapping her cheek briskly and saying, 'Stay with me! Stay with me!' each time she started dozing. Then to the amazement of all the midwives, he keeled over and passed out as soon as the baby was born!

As soon as one memorable couple walked through the

door, it was obvious that she was the practical one in the relationship. The husband was a university professor and while he was highly intelligent, he didn't possess much in the way of common sense. As her labour progressed, he turned out to be no use whatsoever to her. He stood there helplessly and didn't have a clue about how to comfort his wife or do anything to help her. Eventually, as much to stop him standing there like a spare part as anything else, I said to him, 'Open up your wife's bag, take out a flannel, wet it and then mop her brow.'

He obediently rummaged around in the bag of baby clothes, took out a flannel, wet it and then proceeded to mop his own forehead with it! In between her increasingly painful contractions his wife kept shaking her head.

'I told you. He's got absolutely *no* common sense,' she said.

At one time there was a theory that stimulating a woman's nipples could help the uterus contract after birth. One dad, who was very keen to be proactively involved in the whole process, actually sat behind his wife and did just that after she'd given birth, explaining to us that he was trying to help the uterus contract. I've no idea whether this particular technique does or doesn't work, but this was something that none of the staff had ever seen before and there were certainly a few raised eyebrows amongst us!

In parenting classes we teach breathing techniques for

both the women and their partners to use during labour. Women are very strong, often stronger than they think, and are able to support themselves during labour with the aid of things like good breathing techniques. After the birth of their baby, many men say that the relaxation and breathing really worked for them and that they had both used these techniques during the birth. Sometimes they can embrace the whole thing a bit too enthusiastically, though – I know of one man who was so chilled out he fell asleep in the breathing class ... and his snores prevented the heavily pregnant women around him from relaxing at all!

Partners are generally a fantastic asset to have in the delivery room. They can be a real advocate for the women – they know what they like and they can encourage them to keep going a little bit longer. They can also act as a conduit between the woman and the midwife and I'm often really impressed by the level of trust that exists between a really supportive couple.

Of course, not all partners are supportive and we try to manage whatever relationship issues seem to be going on in the room. We would try to get the partner on side if it was felt that they were not being supportive, but at the end of the day we're not there as a relationship counsellor but to provide clinical care. Sometimes we do get a sixth sense that the relationship between the couple is not a healthy one. Now and again a midwife comes out of the delivery room and says that the man has an intimidating presence that made her feel uncomfortable. In those cases, the midwife would try to get the woman on her own and ask her if everything is okay although that can be difficult if the man doesn't leave the woman's side.

Midwives are great observers of relationships. We develop an instinct about what couples' relationships are like and how robust they are or are not. It's much harder for couples to manipulate a situation around birth and put on an act. Birth is an honest, naked situation and there's no getting away from that. People's emotions at the time of birth are so raw that they're not able to hide their true selves.

It's routine for midwives who look after women during their pregnancy to ask if there are any problems with domestic violence, along with questions about alcohol and substance abuse. Domestic violence does increase in pregnancy and while the midwives' role is to provide clinical care, we are increasingly aware of the wider social responsibilities we have. We have a finite window of opportunity to help women get the help they need and the opportunity to explore things that might get women out of a particular hole. A lot of our role is about understanding that we can help women with wider problems that they might be experiencing.

A woman will sometimes confide in a midwife, even if it's some time after she's given birth. Late one Friday evening, one of our midwives had a call from a woman she'd looked after some time before. The midwife had suspected at the time that something wasn't right, and now the woman confessed she had fled her violent husband with the children but didn't know what to do. In cases like these we would immediately involve social services and help the woman to access the support she needed. I think it's a testament to the bond that can develop during labour that this distressed woman chose to confide in her midwife.

Labour is obviously all about the woman, but it can also be a difficult time for the man. Often it's the first time in his life that he's seen the woman he loves in such agony. Although he's responsible for getting her pregnant and so has a large stake in the birth, he can often feel completely helpless when she's in labour. He might not be sure of the correct 'labour etiquette'. His partner can be rude, intolerant and keen on hurling obscenities in his direction. Not surprisingly, he's worried about saying or doing the wrong thing and aggravating an already delicate situation.

While dads can be a fantastic help in the delivery room, they are never centre stage – more of a sideshow to the main event. They're not the people we pay the most attention to. We don't want them to feel left out, but our attention is absolutely on the mother. Sometimes the man will just sit uncommunicatively in the corner with his newspaper up, and some men just aren't particularly empathetic and can't see what all the fuss is about. On the other hand, some dads can really lighten up a tense atmosphere in the delivery room. One of our midwives looked after a woman whose partner worked as a Tarzan stripogram for a living ...

'He was short and bald and very kind and funny – not the likeliest looking Tarzan,' she told us afterwards over a cuppa. 'He did his entire routine for me in the delivery room, but thank the Lord he didn't actually strip!'

Funnily enough we do get partners stripping off sometimes – if their wife is having a pool birth and they want to get in with her. We do ask them not to take absolutely *all* their clothes off though. I remember one man who got into the water in a brand-new black tee-shirt. The dye ran everywhere and turned the water black ... and that was the end of his wife's water birth. She and her husband had to make a pretty hasty exit from the pool and the baby was delivered 'on dry land'.

Men sometimes come out with the most hilarious things. During parent education classes we do little quizzes with the parents-to-be, giving them various problems and asking them how they would deal with them. One of the problems is 'not enough milk'. Women respond to this with suggestions about how to improve the flow of their breast milk, while men proudly come up with suggestions like, 'pop down to the garage and buy an extra pint'.

One of my colleagues was looking after a woman who arrived in the unit in the middle of the night in strong labour. She was hanging onto the man by her side for dear life, and even during her strongest contractions refused to let go of him. The midwife was impressed with the extremely deep and close bond that the couple had, for the woman wanted to have physical contact with him all the way through labour. Some women, even when they love their partner very much, don't want him getting too close. While the woman screamed the man was quiet, but stayed stoically by her side, and looked really concerned every time she shouted out in pain.

There was a very joyful atmosphere in the room and a huge sense of relief when the baby was born fit and well with a strong, lusty cry.

'Congratulations, it's a boy!' declared the midwife, cradling the baby. 'Would you like to have your first cuddle with your brand new baby, dad?' she asked, turning to the man.

'Oh ... no! No, no thanks,' he stuttered, taking a step back. 'I'm not the dad, I'm just the taxi driver who brought her here. I've never seen her before in my life!' he said, laughing.

'Why didn't you say something?' asked the midwife.

'Well, she needed me. I didn't feel I could just walk away and leave her by herself. Now I need to go and clean out my taxi!' He smiled at the woman, wished her good luck and made a hasty exit. We wondered if the two of them stayed in touch afterwards, having shared such a seminal moment. You must always expect the unexpected in this job!

8

EARLY ARRIVALS

Parents get very excited about certain occasions – like when a baby first opens its eyes and when a baby has its first poo ... everyone gets very excited about this poo that's come out, whereas for a full-term baby that would just be a normal process. On the neo-natal unit, when you're watching for every event, something like that is monumental.

Fiona, episode 7

MARIA

The most common reason babies end up in the neo-natal unit is because they are born too soon. Of course we do look after poorly full-term babies as well, but the majority of neo-natal unit babies are premature and have not developed sufficiently to survive in the world without the sort of assistance that state-of-the-art medical technology can provide. Sometimes babies are born premature because they have a particular health problem in the womb – which may or may not have been detected on the ultra-sound scan that all pregnant women are routinely given – but a lot of the time there's no explanation when a woman goes into spontaneous, premature labour. All the ante-natal tests may have indicated that everything was going well, but then her contractions suddenly start a few months before the baby is due. Babies who are born early don't tend to hang around – it's not as tight a squeeze for them to get out of their mother's body as it is for a full-term baby and because they're so tiny the cervix doesn't even need to be completely dilated to allow them to pass through.

I've had the privilege of delivering a baby at twenty-four weeks, still wrapped in the sac of amniotic fluid it developed in, so it was completely protected and cushioned and didn't have too traumatic a birth experience. It's very strange to see such a tiny baby born like that. It doesn't look quite human.

Premature birth is usually an unexpected event and even without grappling with the health problems a pre-mature baby is likely to have, parents are in a total state of shock that the baby they were looking forward to welcoming into the world several months hence has emerged so early. It's important to sit down and talk gently to the parents about what has happened and what is likely to happen next. The mum might not be able to do the things that she would expect to be able to do for her new baby, like breastfeeding, and it's likely that they won't even be able to hold and cuddle their son or daughter. This can be incredibly difficult for parents to come to terms with.

Premature babies often need oxygen. They need to be kept in an incubator to control their temperature and if they're very premature they won't be able to feed by the conventional route. Instead they'll either be fed through a nasal gastric tube or through a line into their heart or bloodstream. All of these measures are interventionist – they're put in place to try to give the baby a better chance of surviving, but they do risk creating irritation and infection.

Having their tiny babies surrounded by so many beeping machines is very scary for parents. Without any warning or preparation, they have entered an alien and terrifying world in which their precious child is struggling to survive. Understandably they're in a state of extreme anxiety. When a woman has given birth to a normal, healthy baby on the labour ward, she will usually have lots of happy, excited visitors afterwards who arrive bearing various kinds of gifts. The parents, family and friends all celebrate the new arrival together. In stark contrast, the neo-natal ward is an environment where friends and family are kept to an absolute minimum. Their baby's birth has not been the happy occasion they had expected and they cannot rejoice in the same way as parents who have a full-term, healthy baby. We can only celebrate each little milestone, as a step along the way to what everyone hopes will be a full recovery.

In the first few weeks of the life of a baby in the neo-natal unit, the conversations we have with parents are filled with caveats because no one knows quite how things are going to develop. Parents are always on the edge of their seats when their child – however old he or she is – is ill, but parents of babies in the neo-natal unit are constantly standing on the edge of a precipice.

The staff in the neo-natal unit have a very tough job to do. The work is very intensive and if a baby has been there for a while they can get very involved with it and its parents. Supporting parents is a big part of the work of neo-natal staff and relationships forged there are very different from those which develop on labour ward before and after the birth of a healthy baby. In the neo-natal unit, the staff must prop up and provide emotional support for parents, and everyone rejoices together when the babies make good progress and become well enough to go home with their parents.

We encourage parents to allow themselves to be cautiously optimistic about the baby and about their chances of having more babies who will be perfectly healthy. We know that if the woman gets pregnant again both parents are likely to be terrified as inevitably their fears about what happened with the premature birth will always be super-imposed on any later pregnancy.

When a woman goes into labour prematurely, we will try to do everything we can to stop that labour in its tracks and keep the pregnancy going for as long as possible, and there are various things we can try. The waters may spontaneously rupture, but as long as the woman keeps producing amniotic fluid we will try to keep the pregnancy going.

Meconium liquor is where the baby's bowels open before it's born, which can be a sign of distress. This has varying degrees of significance, depending on how close to the birth it occurs. The closer it is to the birth the less worrying it is, but my heart always sinks a little bit when I see it. If we see meconium we would aim to stop the baby taking a breath, because if it is in its mouth it can go into the lungs and cause a lot of damage.

When I was a student, a midwife asked for permission to deliver her daughter's baby in one of our birth centres, which is in the New Forest. Permission was given and when the time came, the labour was progressing normally. But at the beginning of the second stage of labour, there was evidence of meconium. As the birth was so close they decided to remain at the centre, rather than transferring into the main hospital. Unfortunately it soon became clear that the situation was worse than they had anticipated, and as the baby was born it became apparent that it had taken meconium into its lungs. Following an emergency transfer into the main hospital, the baby was admitted into the neo-natal unit where it was ventilated and sadly eventually died. It's a very unhappy story and was just one of those awful things that you remember because it was so rare an event.

A girl of fifteen gave birth to a baby who needed care in the neo-natal unit. She was with her partner who was a similar age to her. There are so many stereotypes about feckless, teenage mums but I have rarely met such thoughtful, capable parents as this couple – they were just fantastic. They doted on their baby and showed great maturity about the whole situation. When the young father held the baby in his arms for the first time, the delight on his face was a wonderful thing to witness. They were determined to support their tiny baby as well as they could, and to face head-on whatever challenges lay ahead of them. This young couple were very matter-of-fact about life – as far as they were concerned this was their special baby and they were going to come through this situation. The mum didn't need coaxing, like some mums of babies in the neo-natal unit do, to change her baby's nappy and wash it. It was so refreshing to see how proactive both of these parents were. The baby was with us for a very long time before it was well enough to go home and I got to know the couple very well. They taught me a lot about how we, as professionals, do sometimes have a tendency to stand in judgment over others. If we do this, we are doing a terrible injustice to people.

An important part of the work of neo-natal unit staff is to get the parents to bond with their babies. Their baby is in an incubator and there are nine other cots with sick babies in them. The fact that the baby is ill and is hooked up to the latest hi-tech equipment means there are real physical barriers to parents who are trying to bond with their new baby. The baby was probably whisked away immediately after the birth to be stabilised and they won't have had that opportunity to hold the baby, gaze into its eyes and count its fingers and toes the way parents of healthy babies can.

The first time parents venture into the neo-natal unit they are embarking on a steep learning curve. The first thing that hits them is the warmth of the unit. The equipment generates a lot of heat and the babies need the room temperature to be very warm to mimic the conditions inside the womb. There are all kinds of noises, too, with the intermittent beeping of machines and various alarms going off, indicating a variation in temperature or oxygen levels in one or more of the babies. All this can be very intimidating for parents.

Once parents have got past some of this cumbersome machinery they're shown to their baby's incubator and lying there, barely visible, is their tiny child, resembling a little bird, all wrapped up. The incubator has two portholes and the parents might not even be able to see their baby's face because there's a tube attached to it. Instead of the beautiful pink, bouncing baby they had been anticipating holding in their arms in a few months, time, they've got this tiny, translucent thing.

Of course, the parents are very upset to have a baby who is so fragile and unwell, and they often panic.

'What do I do? Is this really my baby?' they say to each other. This is not what they thought their precious baby would look like. When a nurse asks them if they'd like to change their baby's nappy, they are often completely over-whelmed with anxiety.

'Which bit do I touch? Will I hurt the baby if I touch it?' Because it's probably the first time they've seen their baby properly, a member of staff has to introduce them to their child and reassure them about which bits they can and can't touch. It's so hard for mums not being able to hold the baby they've given birth to.

I can't think of many areas of medicine that are more challenging in terms of providing care to the parents and developing a trusting relationship to them than the neo-natal unit. Midwives who work on labour ward don't get involved with the women and their partners over a long period of time, but on the neo-natal ward it's different. The staff get to know the parents well over a period of weeks or months, and they're aware of the many problems that can emerge.

Every aspect of having a baby in the neo-natal unit is incredibly stressful for couples. If the parents have older children at home there is an enormous amount of pressure to organise care for them as well as the practicalities of having to go back to work after the birth. My own husband doesn't like hospitals very much and I don't know how he would have coped if he had had to come in every day. Men can find that environment and the fragility of the babies particularly difficult.

Of course, for some babies, the mood is positive right from the start. If the prognosis is good and they only need to spend a short time in the unit before going home, every-one is optimistic and the time spent in the neo-natal unit isn't too traumatic – it's just a stepping stone before parents take home their healthy baby. Some babies do make fantastic progress and move on really quickly. But for other parents the whole experience is much more of a roller-coaster, and even when the baby is healthy enough to go home, they feel enormous anxiety. If a baby has spent a long time in the unit, it can be scary for parents to take it home – they can't imagine how on earth they'll manage to look after the baby without the support of the neo-natal unit staff. We do try and give parents a couple of nights in the hospital looking after their baby before they take it home, as a sort of dry run.

Expressing milk is one of the most positive things a mum can do while her baby's in the unit, because the milk can be stored and fed to the baby when required. This simple thing can give the mother a real sense of achievement when all else seems to be falling apart. For some mums, even if it's a long time before their baby can feed from the breast, they feel really proud that it's their milk getting to their baby through a tube, rather than formula milk. We have had some really excellent successes where babies have been in the unit for a long time and then go home and are successfully breastfed.

The atmosphere on the neo-natal unit is very supportive and some of the parents strike up friendships with each other because they're all spending so much time there, and they are going through similar experiences. Sometimes however, unconscious rivalries can emerge between parents who are all anxiously measuring the progress of their sick babies. I remember when we had two very poorly babies in the unit, one born at twenty-four weeks and the other at twenty-eight weeks. At the beginning, the twenty-four-weeker did better than the slightly older baby. The parents were all lovely and built up a friendship with each other. They were all in a state of shock because none had any warning that their babies were going to be born prematurely. Then the twenty-eight-weeker overtook the younger baby, and there was definitely a bit of gentle sparring between them. Happily, both of the babies were eventually well enough to go home and both mums went on to have a second healthy baby.

There is a huge variation in the kinds of babies who pass through the neo-natal unit. We might have a baby born at thirty-five weeks who we're just keeping an eye on to ensure that its temperature remains stable. In those situations we can be very positive and optimistic. It's completely different from the case of a twenty-four-week baby whose eyes are still fused shut. In those cases, we know the journey ahead is going to be a tough one. With these babies we try to be optimistic about the tiniest things, because we want to boost the parents as much as we can.

'It's fantastic that you've expressed that breast milk, he'll really enjoy that ... How lovely that you're stroking your baby so he knows you're here,' we say. We comment on the little details like a baby kicking or clenching its tiny hands around one of their parent's fingers. We show parents how to wash their baby with a cotton wool ball and explain to them how much the baby likes the sound of their parents' voices. Staff take a detailed history of what the baby has been doing during the day, so that even if the parents can't be there all the time, they don't miss out on any positive progress. When we have to deliver bad news, we try to couch it in positive terms if at all possible.

'The baby didn't have such a good morning. His heart slowed down, but now it seems to have picked up again,' is one way of delivering gloomy news. Bradycardia is when the baby's heartbeat slows right down but doesn't actually stop. In these cases gently touching the baby can get it going again. If it nearly stops, there will be lots of activity amongst staff to stabilise the heart and that can be really frightening for parents.

A member of staff will shout, 'I need some help here!' and a swarm of people gather around the incubator. The baby is placed on the resuscitaire, while the parents look on in horror, thinking that this could be the end of the road for their child. Once the baby is stabilised, it's put back into the incubator. We try and lighten the mood a bit for parents by saying, 'What a naughty boy. You need to speak sternly to your son, don't let him do that again!'

A lot of pregnant women worry about miscarrying in the first twelve weeks, but if they get past that point they often assume they will go on to have a normal, full-term baby. So it's shocking for them when that doesn't happen and also for midwives, too, because even if there are additional risk factors we still anticipate that mother and baby will both be fine. Mothers are simply not prepared for giving birth early and having their baby cared for in the neo-natal unit. A baby needs the nine months to develop and usually won't go home until it's reached full-term or more.

When a baby is born too early and is very unwell, the question the medical team ask is, 'Will this baby have an opportunity to live?'

The degree of prematurity of a baby isn't the only

indicator of the long-term outlook. Babies born at twenty-four weeks sometimes do better than babies born four weeks later. A baby who does quite well at first and then deteriorates might not do as well as a baby who starts off less well but then makes steady progress. Most will require oxygen therapy and support with feeding and you know they're moving along a very long, winding path. A baby who has not had a brain bleed is likely to do better than one who has, because there isn't that significant interference with their development. Babies who have small bleeds may have some interference with their physical or mental development, but it might not become apparent until they go to school. Babies that are very premature can have long faces even as adults, as a result of the way they lie in the incubators – although these days we cushion their heads more. It can be very obvious, when a baby's condition has deteriorated and we can't get it off the ventilator, that there has been a significant deterioration of the lungs or the gut. A point does come where you say, 'This isn't going to work and we can't continue prolonging this life'.

It's very tough when that happens because, of course, you never want to have that conversation with parents. Wherever possible we try to give parents realistic hope, but when we've done everything we can and know that there's no longer a reasonable chance that the baby will survive, we have to say that we've come to the end of the road.

Because there is so much more that neo-natal technology can do now, it can be hard for parents to accept that there is nothing more we can do for their baby and that we have to let nature take its course. When parents are told that their baby has significant brain damage, it can be very hard to accept this reality, because *all* tiny babies are helpless and reliant on parents for their survival. But as a premature baby with brain damage grows into a child, a teenager and then an adult, significant and complex problems begin to emerge. It's really hard to paint that picture for parents, because all they can see is life and death, rather than that really tough picture in the middle. And they want to avoid the death option at all costs.

While the loss of any baby is a terribly sad event for all the neo-natal staff, the doctors, nurses and midwives involved in these cases do, understandably, have a different perspective from the parents. They sometimes say it's a blessing that that baby died, because they know and understand only too well what a terrible struggle life will be for a baby with significant disabilities.

Our instinct is always to fight for life, but as professionals we need to keep a sense of perspective about what is achievable and what is realistic. From what I've seen, the staff in the neo-natal unit know when to say, 'no more'. When a baby has major problems and needs frequent resuscitation, you have to think to yourself, 'What am I bringing back?' Life is terribly fragile and we must remember that the first rule of medicine is always to do no harm.

The neo-natal staff are wonderful at making the last few hours as good as they can be for the parents and their baby. We take them all into a quiet room. All the tubes are removed, and often it's the first time they have held the baby without tubes.

When I joined the neo-natal unit there was a little boy who had been born shortly before I arrived. He was very premature and was making very little progress. His mother had had a long period of infertility and various treatments before when she became pregnant with him. Sadly he was born too early and, for a long time, his progress was a case of three steps forward and twenty steps back. He really was a poorly baby and I don't remember him ever smiling. It was an enormous struggle for him and his parents to get anywhere near the point that most parents can take for granted: having a healthy, happy baby.

His parents came in every day to see him and were absolutely lovely. He had several episodes where his heart rate slowed down but we always managed to stabilise it again. It must have been incredibly difficult for his parents to witness this fragile scrap of a baby suffering so many different health crises. But somehow they always managed to stay cheerful.

He was about six months old when he was finally well

enough to leave the unit and go home, supported by oxygen. I remember his parents excitedly going up to London to buy him some of the things he'd need when he came home. After a long struggle, he had finally started growing and doing very well. But then he suddenly had a full-blown cardiac arrest. The whole medical team rushed to his side and tried to bring him back, but the resuscitation attempts failed and there comes a point in these episodes when you have to say 'no more'. It was a terrible loss for his parents who had struggled so hard to conceive him, and been so brave since his birth. We were all heartbroken; we had developed a strong attachment to him because we had cared for him over such a long period of time and had got to know his parents so well. After his death, a few of us ran a half-marathon to raise money for the neo-natal unit. We used to meet after work to train – we weren't much good at running, but we did complete the race, finishing at the same time as the competitors in wheelchairs.

I was young and idealistic when this little boy died, and I really wanted to make a positive difference. You expect older people to die, but when it's babies in the neo-natal unit, it's a completely different story. His death really made me think about the cruelty of life. His mum wrote a letter to every single member of staff, with a photo of her son attached, recalling personal anecdotes about how that particular member of staff had helped him. It was a lovely and very touching thing to receive. In the letter she wrote to me, the little boy's mum explained how lucky she felt to have had a few months with him. If I was looking for role-model parents, this couple would be them. They were completely there for him and had been prepared to accept him on any terms. They were just incredibly pleased to be his parents. His death had a big impact on me.

Any death is very sad but when it's such a tiny baby, there's an acute sense of sadness thinking about the life he could have led.

ROS

One of the areas where medical technology has really developed is in the field of neo-natal medicine. Yet despite all these fantastic advances, there are still so many things that we can't do and don't understand. There are times when I'm looking after a woman in labour and the trace on the baby's heartbeat is giving cause for concern. There's great consternation amongst the members of the medical team, but then the baby emerges pink and healthy and everybody's panic dissipates as quickly as an ice cream left out in the sun.

'What was that all about?' we ask each other, relieved but puzzled nonetheless.

We had one baby who was born in a really poor condition and was whisked straight off to the neo-natal unit. It didn't do at all well and the medical team decided to withdraw treatment because they felt there was no hope for the baby. They prepared the parents for the worst, but miraculously the baby picked up and thrived after they withdrew treatment. Nobody could explain how this could happen, but we were all just incredibly happy and rejoiced with the parents.

Some premature babies arrive very quickly. One minute there's nothing happening and then suddenly a woman's waters break and she gets the urge to push. Before you know it you've got a tiny baby in your hands, and it's being whisked onto the resuscitaire straight away. Often these babies don't cry or breathe immediately, and the paediatrician has to put a tube down the baby's throat to get it to breathe. There isn't that reassuring hearty cry that is music to our ears at the birth of a healthy baby. Everyone huddles round the resuscitaire, trying to do what they can for the baby. When a baby is born prematurely, we're always pleased if it's a girl, because girls seem to do better than boys, although I don't know why.

If a woman comes in, is having some contractions and showing signs that she might be going into labour, there's a test we can do that involves taking a swab from the cervix which can predict whether or not she's likely to go into labour in the next two weeks. If we know a woman is going to go into premature labour, we give her steroid injections to help mature the baby's lungs – premature lungs are quite stiff and hard to inflate and the injections can help. If we give the injections and the woman doesn't go into labour, that's not a problem and the injections won't have harmed the baby in any way. A woman who is considered to be at risk of going into premature labour might be put on bed rest – either at home, or in the hospital where she can be monitored more closely.

The level of risk often depends on what stage the baby is born at. If it's born at twenty-four weeks there are all sorts of complications but if the baby is born at thirty-two weeks we would expect it to be of reasonable size although it might need extra oxygen and feeding because the suck reflex won't have developed fully. Unless there are other complications, we would expect thirty-two-week babies to do well. Babies born at twenty-four or twenty-five weeks are on the borderline of viability. The age of viability was brought down from twenty-eight to twenty-four weeks because we were getting more babies surviving at twenty-four weeks. If a woman comes in at twenty-three weeks, there are decisions to be made about the baby's prognosis, its life expectancy and its long-term health problems. The neo-natal team have to counsel the parents about what the baby's chances are and how much resuscitation is appropriate. A lot depends on the weight of the baby when it's born – a good size baby born at twenty-three or twenty-four weeks has a better prognosis than a smaller one born at the same age.

Very premature babies are difficult for everyone. Parents want everything possible to be done for their baby and aren't always in the right state of mind to think clearly about what the cost of survival might be in terms of the baby's quality of life. As health professionals our whole ethos is focused on saving lives, so making a decision that it's not appropriate to carry on resuscitating one of these tiny babies is a really difficult one to make.

The premature baby is monitored closely for the first few hours or days of its life and then a decision is made about whether or not it is viable to continue with treatment. The whole thing is incredibly emotional. Doctors have to make a decision about whether or not the problems that these tiny babies have are compatible with life, and what sort of long-term disabilities the child is going to have.

The idealised images people see in the media and on television do encourage us to expect perfection in every area of life – we need to have a perfect car, a perfect house, a perfect holiday and a perfect baby, too. Yet we all know wonderful, happy children with mental or physical disabilities and we can't imagine them not being here.

There are no easy answers to these kinds of life-or-death issues and guiding couples through the decision-making process is very hard. As midwives we can present them with the facts but we have to remain impartial and non-judgmental. The decisions are for them to make.

Some women who give birth prematurely might be very ill themselves, with severe pre-eclampsia, for example. They might be too unwell to see their baby immediately, which creates additional emotional stress. In those cases her partner may take photos so that at least the woman has some sense of the baby she's just given birth to.

Pre-eclampsia is a condition peculiar to pregnancy. It's a reaction to the pregnancy and is more common in young girls and women experiencing their first pregnancy. If there's a family history of pre-eclampsia, then there's more chance of a woman developing it. We try to control the blood pressure with drugs but if we can't, and the woman's blood pressure becomes uncontrollable, it can stop the baby from growing. As the blood pressure increases, the woman's hands, feet and brain swell. She develops brisk reflexes, responding very strongly when a knee or other joint is touched. At this point she's at risk of having a pre-eclamptic fit. The only cure for pre-eclampsia is delivering the baby. With some women their blood pressure doesn't start creeping up until thirty-four to thirty-five weeks. Others have no history of high blood pressure but at twenty-eight or twenty-nine weeks their blood pressure suddenly goes through the roof. If that happens the baby needs to be delivered as soon as possible.

For some women the blood-pressure drugs work, and for others they don't. We have to check these women's blood pressure more frequently which makes them more anxious and if their blood pressure is high, they have to stay overnight which is hard if they have other children. Many couples experiencing a first pregnancy don't want to be sep-arated overnight, but if there's a clinical need to keep the woman in hospital under observation they have no choice but to be separated. Wherever possible we try to monitor women in the community, but sometimes they need to be observed more closely.

Birth can be one of the most joyous parts of life, but seeing the suffering of babies that need neo-natal care and the devastating effect the whole thing has on their parents is one of the saddest parts of our job. If I've been involved in a case where the baby's been taken off to the neo-natal unit, after the shift I go over and over in my mind whether I could have done anything differently.

9

TRIUMPH AGAINST THE ODDS

It's not enough to like babies; you've got to be a people person. Because it's not just learning the clinical skills and understanding the mechanism of pregnancy and childbirth, it's being able to support women emotionally, because they come in with all their baggage – y'know not just their suitcase and their pillows – but the emotional stuff, the relationship stuff, what they've learned growing up . . . so you have to be able to deal with all those things as well. And every input you make is important.

Ros, episode 6

ROS

Ante-natal screening is really good now, so I'm happy to say that we rarely get babies born with unexpected problems.

And thanks to medical advances, a lot of the problems that do arise can easily be resolved.

There are two conditions that can't be picked up on ultrasound scans – cleft palate and club foot. But even these can be corrected very effectively with surgery a few months after the birth of the baby. Nevertheless, I really feel for a couple when their baby is born with a cleft palate. It can be shocking and disappointing when they don't have the beautiful baby they were expecting. However, it's good to be able to reassure them that it's a problem that is quite straightforward to sort out.

I've done a few shoulder dystocia deliveries. This is when the baby's head is delivered but the shoulder gets stuck. This is an emergency and there are various manoeuvres we can do to try to get the baby out so that it can start breathing. The important thing in these cases is to get as much help as you can as quickly as possible. Once there's a medical team in the room, we have to try each of the recognised manoeuvres for this condition for thirty seconds, before moving onto the next. In a situation like this, that can feel like a very long time. After each manoeuvre, the atmosphere gets really tense. We once had a baby with a swollen abdomen who got stuck. We weren't sure whether the baby was going to survive or not, but thankfully it did after the doctor managed to turn it in a corkscrew-like movement, which successfully freed the shoulder. We are all acutely aware of how much responsibility we have in life-or-death cases like that, but in times of emergency the training kicks in and we just get on with the job.

In one shoulder dystocia case our hearts were in our mouths because there was a five-minute delay between the head and the rest of the body being delivered. The baby was a large one. The room was full of medics and we went through almost every possible manoeuvre to try to get the baby out. When we eventually managed it, there were huge sighs of relief all round. As well as the risks to the mother and baby, it's also very distressing both for the mother and for the father watching the whole thing, and it's important that some of the staff in the room are offering support to them as well as dealing with the clinical side.

These days when you press the emergency buzzer staff come running within seconds from all directions, but fifteen or twenty years ago things were much more laid back. Sometimes we would be dealing with a post-partum haemorrhage – there would be blood everywhere and the midwife might be trying to get a drip into the woman with one hand while keeping the other clamped firmly on the woman's uterus to try to stop the bleeding. At that point an anaesthetist, generally a man, would wander in and ask, casually, 'What's the woman's blood pressure?' The midwives would look at him aghast. How on earth would they have had time to take a woman's blood pressure when dealing with an emergency like that? The anaesthetists seemed to assume that midwives had more hands than an octopus!

The biggest baby I've delivered weighed 12 lb 6 oz. To everyone's surprise it emerged very normally. The mum lay on her left side, which worked well and she only had a tiny tear.

We had one woman who was very overweight and was in labour with her first baby. We were really hoping that she would be able to avoid having a Caesarean – this kind of surgery is much harder to perform on a large woman as there are a lot of layers of fat to cut through and there's more chance of infections developing in the folds of her skin than there is in a slimmer woman. So I was relieved that she was pushing really well. There were lots of doctors and nurses in the room, just in case things went wrong and she had to be rushed down to theatre. She had a really good attitude and a great sense of humour. Everyone was cheering her on and there was absolute elation in the room when she pushed out a huge twelve-pound baby successfully. Cases like this are so satisfying. Helping a woman achieve a normal delivery in very difficult circumstances is a really fantastic feeling.

MARIA

One of my colleagues, Tina Parker, looked after a woman who could not conceive naturally because her husband had a low sperm count. She did not have any physical problems herself, and they were able to have IVF, successfully, with donor sperm, and gave birth to a healthy baby boy.

After several years, they decided they would like to try for another child but had a failed IVF cycle which was very emotionally draining and stressful for the whole family. Their son by this time was nine years old and very aware of what was happening. They were notified that the frozen sperm they'd used to conceive their first son would expire after ten years, and they were keen to try again using the same sperm because they wanted their next child to have similar features to their first. Sadly, their second IVF attempt with this sperm was not successful. But the woman was absolutely determined to have another baby. She longed to experience a birth and breastfeeding once again, and to have a larger family. She and her husband eventually decided to try for a third time with different sperm.

The woman received a call from her fertility clinic with details of the characteristics of the men who had donated sperm that could be used for their next treatment. What a bizarre phone call! She was given a list of eye and hair colours to choose from, as if picking from a menu. The whole thing felt very detached and unreal, but she knew that it was just one more necessary step on the road towards having another baby.

The commitment and dedication required to undergo IVF treatment is huge. It involves a rollercoaster of emotion, often a significant financial commitment, clinical procedures, hospital visits and anticipation, along with the constant, gnawing anxiety that the treatment will fail. Happily, on this occasion, the treatment resulted in a successful twin pregnancy.

The woman longed for a positive birth experience. Early on in her pregnancy she suffered badly with sickness and tiredness, but remained determined to be treated as a 'normal' woman having a 'normal' pregnancy and birth. She worked closely with her consultant and Tina to ensure that all the care plans were agreed by her and that decisions weren't taken by the clinicians over her head. Her empowerment was remarkable.

She drew up a flexible birth plan, which included recommendations from her consultant. She really wanted to have her babies at home, but he strongly recommended a hospital birth for her. As the pregnancy progressed, she reconciled herself to a Caesarean section if one was needed. She had two birth plans, one for a normal birth and one for a theatre delivery.

What she really wanted was control of her situation whichever way her labour and birth went. She met with Tina, another midwife and a midwifery supervisor to prepare for the birth. They explained procedures, guidelines, recommendations from her consultant, and discussed the role of her partner and her son, both of whom were going to be in the birth room. They were keen to be as supportive as possible. The woman's birth plan was circulated and all the labour coordinators, theatre staff, doctors and midwifery supervisors were made aware of it.

She went into spontaneous labour one evening when she was thirty-eight weeks pregnant. Both of her babies had their heads down and were in the right position for a normal delivery. Both had grown well. Tina stayed with her in the early stage of labour at home until she was ready to move to the hospital. She had opted for a pool birth and the medical team was on standby, keeping their fingers crossed that she would have a normal delivery.

She laboured quietly in the pool with her husband supporting her and her son nearby playing an electronic game. Tina was in the room with her, and an emergency team on standby in case anything went wrong. A few minutes before midnight she got the urge to push and glanced at the clock. She could not speak but the medical staff knew she was determined that her twins should have the same birthday. At one minute past midnight she started pushing and her first daughter was born in the pool.

The atmosphere in the room was electric. Everybody wept tears of joy. She and the baby had skin-to-skin contact, whilst everyone waited for the second baby. She handed the first baby to her husband and then decided to step out of the pool. The midwives made her comfortable on a birth stool. She rested against her husband who handed the first daughter to her brother to hold. He sat very still while he was holding her and had his first conversation with his sister. He seemed very relaxed and was proud of his role as older brother.

Her contractions resumed and the second baby, another daughter, was born safely and handed immediately to her for skin-to-skin contact. Tina made her comfortable reclining on the floor on a big bean bag and gave her both of her newborn daughters to hold. She cried with happiness and so did everyone else in the room. She felt totally and utterly fulfilled. She breastfed her twins throughout the first year of their life and although she was often very tired, she had excellent support from family, friends and neighbours, who brought food and provided general help in the house.

She was euphoric about the birth of her beautiful babies, but was particularly overjoyed that her wishes about the kind of birth she wanted had been listened to and respected. It was against all odds that she conceived the twins and then achieved the normal delivery that she longed for. But she managed it and was extremely contented and fulfilled when she cradled her new little girls in her arms for the first time.

10

SADNESS IN OUR HEARTS

You go into hospital or you have your baby at home, and then you go home afterwards and you have your normal and healthy baby, and that's what everyone ought to have. But that's not always the way it works out...

Fiona, episode 7

MARIA

When a baby is stillborn it hasn't had the opportunity to draw a single breath. Often these babies are perfect little human beings and seeing them makes me feel cheated on their behalf, when I think about the life they could have lived if they'd survived.

When we have a stillbirth on labour ward, or a baby that unexpectedly dies, the mood of all the staff takes a sharp nosedive. I've had a number of young midwives who have come to me, absolutely distraught after the death of a baby. Even if they did everything right, it can be very hard to move on from such tragic events and the sadness stays in our hearts for a long time. But however we might be feeling inside, it's important that we remain calm and professional on the outside.

A baby's death is as special as its birth. The baby has reached the end of its life before birth. In the neo-natal unit it's possible to see a baby's personality start to develop, but with a baby who is stillborn there's nothing to draw on when you're laying it out or dressing it for the parents to see and cuddle for the first and last time. It's like handling a pure, blank piece of paper. It seems odd that an entire complex being has been created for life and yet that opportunity has been snatched away – sometimes inexplicably, if no cause for the stillbirth can be found.

For many parents the loss of a baby is likely to be one of the most frightening and traumatic things that has ever happened to them. These are not normal circumstances and so we can't expect parents to react in a normal way. Overwhelming grief may manifest itself as aggression or anger. In most areas of their lives parents are in control, but in this situation they are not and for some this is very hard to accept. Dads may find it especially hard as they are used to finding solutions to problems. Parents are grieving both for the loss of their child and the future they anticipated having with it. All plans for the future are frozen and they enter a period of limbo.

We have fantastic family-care sisters who support parents through this very challenging situation, helping them to navigate the rollercoaster of emotions that they will experience, and will refer them for further bereavement counselling if it's necessary.

Part of our journey as midwives through the death or stillbirth of a baby is to talk about it amongst ourselves. Did we do the right thing? Was there anything else we could have done? Although it is not our own child that we've lost, we also feel grief when a baby dies. Dealing with the bad experiences is part of becoming a good midwife – it's very tough emotionally, but it's all part of the job. We never forget that sadness and sense of loss, but we have to put it into a different part of our heads so that we can continue with our work.

We scrutinise all the cases where there's been an unexpected outcome. Sometimes we have to accept that the loss of a baby was an act of God, or an act of nature, and not something that could have been prevented by employing the best possible medical skills or the latest technology.

Many midwives, when laying out a dead baby to get it ready for its parents, will talk to it – it feels like a natural thing to do. It's a very emotional experience, putting one of these babies into some clothes to meet its parents.

Dressing a stillborn baby, giving it a name and an identity can help the parents to connect with the baby and deal with the loss. Many parents feel they want to mark the existence of a baby who was stillborn or died soon after birth in a positive way, at the same time as grieving for it. Apart from the terrible sense of loss a stillbirth can make both parents feel worthless – 'Why couldn't I be a parent?' they ask.

Midwives tend to keep in touch with women who've lost babies so that they can look after them next time round with, hopefully, a happier outcome. One woman who was very emotionally fragile was supported by my colleaugue, Eileen. She gave birth to a lovely little girl and proudly brought her into the hospital to show her off to us a few times after the birth, which is always lovely for us. But just before she was six months old, the baby developed a heart infection and tragically died. There are no words when something like that happens. The woman's relationship disintegrated following the death of their baby, which of course made things even more difficult. She was desperate to have another baby and she got pregnant again. That pregnancy was a profound, challenging experience, and she leaned very heavily on Eileen, who had supported her through the first one. She was terrified that this baby would not survive. When she reached thirty-six weeks, Eileen made sure she was on call so that whenever the woman went into labour she could be by her side. The woman had a water birth and clutched a toy belonging to her first daughter throughout her labour. She delivered on all fours and the baby came out still in the sac. There was a very spiritual moment as she dropped the toy and lifted her daughter up out of the water. There was something magical about the moment of the second baby's birth. While it was a terrible tragedy for the woman and her family to have lost her daughter, the midwife who looked after her said that it was a privilege to care for this woman and a very humbling experience. 'I couldn't bring back the baby she lost but at least I could sit there and listen and let her have her voice,' said the midwife. The woman has dedicated herself to raising funds for the hospital's maternity services. That's fantastic for us, it helps her cope with her loss and she says it gives her an opportunity to give something back to the hospital that has given her so much.

Sometimes our service gets extraordinarily busy and it's very challenging to manage things knowing we're so stretched. In my younger days as a midwife working on night duty, I'd be looking after three women at once and would literally be running from room to room, delivering one baby after another. In those days nobody thought twice about it. Now all women in labour receive one-to-one care. There are times when we struggle to provide it and are on the brink of closure, but the quality of care that women receive when they're giving birth has improved dramatically in recent years and safety for women and babies is our number one priority. But however many resources we have, it would be impossible to have perfect outcomes with every single baby we deliver.

Most things are picked up on ultrasound scans these days, but we do still get babies born with abnormalities that weren't evident on the scan. Gastroschisis is a condition where the bowel develops outside the body. It is a condition that can be identified on an ultrasound scan and can usually be treated successfully, although seeing the bowel outside the body can be very distressing for parents. Lisa's baby, Jack, was born with this condition. Watching Lisa's distress as the neo-natal nurse handed Jack – a fragile bundle covered with wires and tubes – to her for the first time was an incredibly emotional scene which moved many people to tears.

There are some conditions that have decreased in frequency thanks to developments in ante-natal care. I haven't seen any cases of spina bifida for years and that's probably because of the introduction of folic acid supplements for pregnant women, which prevent the condition from occurring.

I remember looking after one mother who had a hereditary muscle-wasting disease. She was a carrier and had passed the disease onto her baby who was very badly affected by it. He was a beautiful child, but had very little use of his limbs and was unlikely to ever sit or crawl. The prognosis was not good but she said that she and her partner were determined to have the child and then to deal with whatever followed. Women do make these difficult choices. For some women, when they have a life inside them they're determined to try to preserve that life against all the odds, although caring for a child with a terminal condition is absolutely gruelling, emotionally and physically.

Screening does raise issues for some about the pursuit of perfect babies. Some women, particularly those who are religious, prefer to let nature take its course. They have absolute faith in God and say that what will be will be. There is an argument that we have moved too far towards perfection, losing sight of the fact that the imperfections are the things we should value most. I don't want to live in a perfect world. The imperfections are part of the richness of our existence and it is certainly true that without sadness we cannot appreciate joy.

I'm fortunate to have a fantastic husband who has always been a very good listener; I tend to unwind by going for long walks with the dog. I'm a spiritual person and I do believe in a greater presence. I believe in good and evil and in miracles. Sometimes things are completely inexplicable. I like to think there's a great hand intervening every so often. My husband always says that Christianity has the finest of moral codes and I think there's definitely a sense of well-being that comes with having a faith. People with great faith exude an inner glow. I try to treat people respectfully. I like to rejoice and celebrate and be thankful during times of happiness.

ROS

I'm quite an emotional person and I do find it really hard not to cry in certain situations, such as when a baby is still-born or when a healthy baby is born following a particularly traumatic set of circumstances such as the death of a previous baby. It's hard to know when it's appropriate to show your emotions as a midwife and when it's best to keep them under wraps. Will it help them to see you cry or will it make them feel ten times worse? There's no definite yes or no answer to that question. Every case is different and we have to be guided by our instincts.

I think that the day that I don't feel emotional when a baby is born is the day it's time to stop being a midwife. I feel particularly moved by a birth when I've really bonded with the mother during labour. Witnessing that pure surge of joy when a couple meet their baby for the first time, it's hard not to cry with joy with the parents. When they feel joy, we feel it too.

Occasionally a baby is born in a very bad condition – pale and limp, with a very slow heart rate – but there has been nothing to indicate that there is likely to be a problem during the pregnancy or the labour. When that happens and there have been no prior warning signs, it's a real shock to everyone.

The whole of the clinical team go back over cases like that, effectively retracing our steps to see if there's anything we've missed. Reflection, both as an individual and a team, is very important. When there are emergencies or a bad outcome, it's important for the whole team to discuss them afterwards and see if lessons can be learned. It's also important for everyone involved to be able to get things off their chest and talk to others when something has gone wrong. It's extremely distressing for all the staff when these situations occur and it's important not to keep everything bottled up inside. After cases like that I quite often go home, lie in bed and say over and over to myself, 'Could I have done anything differently? If I had done *a* rather than *b*, would it have changed the outcome in any way?' Questions like that are impossible to answer satisfactorily. Although I'm very experienced, I still think like that every time something goes wrong. Even if I know that there's nothing I could have done that would have changed things, it's impossible not to retrace my steps several times, double and triple checking what I did.

Usually in nursing you're looking after one life, but in childbirth there are two lives at stake and sometimes very difficult choices have to be made. If it's not going to be possible to save both the mother and the child, the priority must be to save the life of the mother. If the mother has a pre-eclamptic fit, it's really important to stabilise her first. When the mother's out of danger, then you consider the baby. In most situations you can save both at the same time, but there are a few occasions where you have to prioritise the mother – make sure that her airway is clear, give her drugs to stop any bleeding, make sure her blood pressure is stable and then decide what the best thing to do with the baby is. It is up to doctors to make these critical decisions in life-or-death situations.

Thankfully I've never been involved in a maternal death, but a nurse I knew well from the gynaecology ward, who was married to an obstetrician, had breast cancer. She became pregnant, and sadly that accelerated her cancer. She was like one of the family to all of us and knowing that she was going to die fairly soon after the birth of her baby was very hard for everyone. But she was determined to have a baby and she got her wish.

If something goes wrong during labour, the midwife pulls the emergency cord to get a lot of people into the room quickly. Often there are a lot of different things that need doing at the same time, and everyone gets on with their part in whatever emergency situation has arisen. To make sure that we keep up to date with the latest safety procedures and technology we have mandatory study days and skills and drills sessions so that everybody can spring into action when a problem occurs. On average there is one problem on every shift, although on one memorable shift we pulled the buzzer six times. By the time we had pressed the buzzer for the final time we felt as if we had experienced pretty much every possible labour scenario. We had a cord prolapse, heavy bleeding, eclamptic fits and an alarming drop in a baby's heart rate. Sometimes a dad presses the emergency buzzer in error thinking that he's pressed the bell to summon the midwife. He looks bemused when the whole emergency team race into the room!

I'm a practising Christian and I think my faith makes me who I am. Being a midwife isn't an easy job, and there are times when I work with people who can be quite difficult. I pray on my way to work that I will be able to make good decisions and choices and that I will be able to be patient and gracious. I try to treat people the way I want to be treated, and try to show love towards them. I strongly believe that God's plan for me was to become a midwife. There are things you can do as a midwife that you can't do as a doctor – I can spend more time with the woman than a doctor can and I can connect more with them. I love that aspect of my job.

Doctors are quite nomadic, especially in their early years, but midwives often tend to stay in the same place for a long time. Certainly there are quite a lot of midwives at the Princess Anne who've worked here for many years. I don't feel old – I still feel as if I'm twenty-five even if some of the other midwives look at me and think I'm ancient. I find that I learn something new with each baby delivered. Recently I delivered a baby for a couple who had lost twins at twenty-seven weeks last year. It was a real privilege to look after the woman when she was in labour. She came into hospital to be induced and I knew she was anxious. When I examined her when she arrived and found the baby's heartbeat she burst into tears of relief.

'Sorry about that, it's just that I'm feeling a bit stressed,' she said. 'Now that I've had a little cry, I'll be fine.'

She was fantastic all the way through her labour and she reminded me of how lucky I am to have had four straight-forward pregnancies. I've seen many women struggle enormously to have one child. It is amazing how resilient human beings can be – I do admire women who can pick themselves up and try again after they've experienced ter-rible tragedies or disappointments. I'm full of admiration for them. Women who have lost a baby never stop grieving for that loss, but giving birth to a healthy baby can soothe the hurt and fill the gap in their lives.

Childbirth is a normal process, not an illness, but things can go wrong, and quite suddenly. We don't want to be doom merchants because the majority of births are straightforward and problem-free, but we can never be blasé. It's our job to always be on the lookout for anything that doesn't seem to be quite right. We use our medical training, the equipment at our disposal and our instincts to make sure we are constantly looking at the whole picture. Listening to the baby's heart, monitoring the woman's contractions and blood pressure and checking for any blood loss is absolutely crucial.

Most women in childbirth are young and healthy and if they suffer blood loss they compensate quite well. But when they can't cope any longer with the amount of blood they're losing, they go into shock. We aim to pick up on problems like blood loss before this happens, and the woman collapses and needs resuscitation. In most cases where something serious arises we can take action to avert disaster.

The first time I looked after a woman who had an eclamptic fit, it was very stressful. I had to do three things at once – look after the mother, look after her baby and alert other staff by pressing the emergency buzzer. My heart was racing and although our training prepares us for these events and tells us the importance of keeping calm, it's almost impossible not to panic inside. When you're caring for a woman in labour, you're looking after two lives rather than one and it's important never to lose sight of that. It really is a huge responsibility. Thankfully the woman and her baby received prompt attention and everything turned out fine in the end.

Witnessing a post-partum haemorrhage for the first time was very shocking. One minute there's no bleeding and the next it's as if someone has turned on a tap full blast. There is a very precise protocol to follow in these situations to stop the bleeding and with prompt action the woman usually makes a good recovery

We often have women phoning labour ward and saying they haven't felt any movement from their baby for a couple of days and we always ask them to come in so we can check them over. Usually everything is fine but sometimes we can't find a heartbeat and it's a total shock to everyone. Understandably some women become absolutely hysterical with grief when confronted with this news. At any stage of the pregnancy it's devastating, but it's hardest when a woman has nearly reached her due date. Women retrace the steps of their pregnancy and start saying, 'if only this or this hadn't happened'. They need an explanation and sometimes they blame us for what has happened, even if the baby died of natural causes – something that no one could have predicted or prevented.

There's very little that we as midwives can say in those situations that will be of any comfort to the bereaved parents apart from, 'I'm really sorry for your loss'. At the point that we have identified that there is no longer a heartbeat, we don't usually know why the baby has died. Sometimes even the post-mortem doesn't reveal a cause of death. The baby who died may have been a big, healthy, perfect baby. It's hard to accept that not everything connected with life and death has a tidy, logical explanation. It is very hard looking after a woman and her partner in these situations because they're so totally overwhelmed by grief.

One of the hardest things for a woman to have to do after receiving such a devastating blow is to go into labour and deliver her dead baby. Once the death has been confirmed with an ultrasound scan, we induce labour with drugs unless it happens spontaneously. The woman sometimes wants the medics to put her to sleep and take the dead baby away by Caesarean, but it's not in her best interests to have major surgery in this sort of case. Understandably, the idea of pushing out a dead baby is horrifying.

Sometimes the baby's death is related to high blood pressure, so the doctors are more involved with monitoring the woman in those cases. One of the doctors signs the baby's death certificate. The doctor counsels the woman and any family members who are with her about the process of induction, when it's going to start and how it's going to happen. If it's a big baby and needs forceps the doctor would be involved in the delivery, otherwise it will be left to the midwife.

These babies can sometimes take a long time to deliver. If the baby has died in the womb at twenty-one or twenty-two weeks, the practicalities of delivery are easier than delivering a big baby at the end of a pregnancy. We give the women as much pain relief as possible and have more options because we don't have to worry about administering drugs that could harm the baby.

Women can have an epidural or a morphine mixture which goes into a syringe. They press a button when they need more pain relief and another dose goes into their veins. Morphine helps to sedate the women as well as helping with the pain. We wouldn't administer a drug like that for a live labour as it could make the baby sleepy.

After the birth, everyone reacts in a different way. Some women don't want to see the baby they've delivered straight away, so we always take photographs. Some parents want them and some don't want to see them immediately, so we put them in her notes so that she can look at them at a later date if she wants to. We also take hand and footprints of the baby to give the parents as many memories as possible. Some want to spend several hours with the baby and don't want to say goodbye.

As midwives we really want to do everything right in those situations. We want to give the parents as much time with the baby as they need and to make the photos look right. There's also a lot of paperwork involved and we must make sure that all the information we record is absolutely correct.

I've looked after a few women who have had stillbirths. Sometimes it's difficult to have a rapport with them because they're understandably very withdrawn. The woman and her partner are focused on comforting each other and I don't want to intrude. Because I don't need to monitor the baby's heartbeat in those circumstances, I try not to be in the room all the time so that I can give them some privacy until the contractions start.

There are two women I did really bond with who were having terminations for medical reasons. In one case the baby was severely affected by spina bifida and in the other the woman's blood pressure was so high it was affecting her life. Her high blood pressure had caused huge damage to the baby and sadly it wasn't growing at all. Neither woman wanted to terminate the pregnancy but they understood why they needed to do so. Both were incredibly strong women and I had huge respect and admiration for them. The woman with pre-eclampsia, which had led to the high blood pressure, was quite ill and was on a lot of drugs to control her condition. I knew that it was unlikely that I'd see her again after the baby had been delivered because she came from a different area and had been referred to our hospital for the termination, but for those few hours that she was in labour, I wanted to give her the best care I possibly could during this major event in her life. The care both women needed was complicated. I was fulfilling my clinical role as a midwife, but also was offering counselling so that both women could talk about how they felt about these sad events. Both had enormous dignity; they weren't angry and they weren't blaming others. They were simply trying to get through a really horrible experience in their lives in the best way that they could. It was a privilege to look after them and was an important learning experience for me to have looked after them well and seen them through to the end of this.

Although the whole thing was terribly sad and traumatic, I felt that I had learned so much from it both as a midwife and a human being. I hope that these experiences make me a better midwife, more able to support other women experiencing these kinds of traumas.

The woman having the termination for the spina bifida baby began bleeding heavily and had to be rushed down to theatre. Following the delivery of the placenta some bits of it were left inside her, which caused the heavy bleeding. It seemed particularly unfair given the sad circumstances of her labour that she had to go through that as well. I managed to remain calm and professional when I was looking after her but when someone else took over from me at the end of my shift all my emotions came out and I just couldn't stop crying.

Thankfully there are always colleagues to talk to after difficult experiences like these and it's much better to talk about it before leaving the hospital rather than carrying it all home with you. Nobody ever questions a midwife crying. This is a very emotional job and raw emotions – both sadness and joy – are always close to the surface. Even when there's a good outcome, this work can be very draining mentally, emotionally and physically. Sometimes I cry with sheer tiredness and then relief that my shift is over if it's been a particularly busy and demanding one. It's good to talk to someone on the shift – if you go home and talk to your family you have to be careful of confidentiality. But

I do talk to my husband about issues that have arisen in general terms. He understands because he's a policeman and he is used to dealing with stressful and traumatic situations too.

I sometimes think to myself, 'I wish I'd done this or that differently,' although in fact it probably wouldn't have made that much difference to the outcome. I worry that a particular midwife might not have got enough support or enough of a break. It's good to talk to another midwife or another coordinator to get things into perspective if it's been a difficult shift. It's also very important to say, 'Thanks for working really hard tonight. I'm glad you understand that we weren't able to give you as many breaks as you should have had.'

I really want to be fair to everybody on the shift and that can be quite hard sometimes. I try to give midwives different things on different shifts so they're not dealing with the same kind of case all the time. You get to know what the midwives' respective strengths are. Some prefer to focus on the one-to-one while others are good at juggling a few cases simultaneously. It's a question of knowing your staff and making the best use of the resources you have.

I aim not to go to sleep with all these issues whizzing around my head. There used to be a canteen at the hospital and at the end of a night shift it was such a treat to occasionally eat a breakfast of bacon and eggs and beans that someone else had cooked and sit and talk about what had gone on in the night. After a carnivorous debriefing like that it was easier to go home, get into bed and sink into a dreamless sleep.

11

HOME BIRTHS AND
OTHER SURPRISES

*I get a buzz out of not knowing what's going to
happen, and not knowing what's going to come in
through the door . . . I like that. I like living life on
the edge . . .*

Fiona, episode 7

ROS

I gave birth to my third and fourth children at home. I'd been disappointed with the first birth that took place in hospital because I had hoped for a natural birth but ended up having various interventions. I loved having my last two children at home – it was just lovely to be in my own surroundings and not to have to leave my family. My fourth child, a daughter, Megan, was born early one morning, and when my husband Simon went to wake the older children up for school he was able to break the news that they had a new sister. They seemed to take the whole thing in their stride but did ask, 'Oh, who was making all that noise?' I had been so focused on pushing that I hadn't been aware I had been making a noise at all! I think women retreat to a different place mentally when they're focused on pushing a baby out.

My oldest daughter, Erica, was eleven when the youngest one was born and she felt very torn about wanting to stay at home with me to help me look after her new sister and racing off to school to break the news to her friends.

The focus of my work has always been in the labour ward but I did do a home birth as a student. I was with a very experienced midwife who was just about to retire. She was a woman who was absolutely brimming with knowledge and common sense. The mum-to-be was a bit of a hippy – very laid-back and seemed to have a lifestyle that was very close to nature. She kept chickens and rabbits in the back garden and her three-year-old daughter showed me the chickens and explained the intricacies of their egg laying cycles. I was very impressed. A future midwife in the making, perhaps! Anyway, happily the labour and birth were very natural and straightforward. One of the lovely things about a home birth is that the new arrival immediately becomes part of the family – something which is delayed for a day or two if the mother gives birth in hospital.

Home birth was common in the fifties and sixties but then waned in popularity. It seems to be making a comeback now, although there are still only a few women who opt for it. Some women only spend a few hours in hospital and then go home, which is a good compromise for them. Occasionally we have women who want to have their babies at home, even when medical advice is strongly urging them to have their baby in hospital. You can't force a woman to come to hospital and we will put a plan in place to try to ensure the safety of the mother and the baby. But in those cases I'm always particularly relieved when I hear that the mother and baby came out of the birth well, even if there was an unscheduled dash to hospital in an ambulance at the last minute.

Sometimes there's a temptation to stereotype women — an assumption that the teenagers will be more immature than the older mums. But in fact some teenage mums are very mature. Seventeen to twenty-five is the optimum physical age to be having babies, and there are some very mature, stable seventeen-year-olds who have a partner and have made a conscious decision to have a baby. Sometimes I've been really surprised by just how emotionally mature sixteen- and seventeen-year-olds can be.

Some teenagers will confide all kinds of intimate details to a midwife but some are shy and embarrassed and don't say very much. Some pull the bed sheets up to their necks, while others are very uninhibited about their bodies and will tell you anything!

MARIA

Young people never fail to surprise me. When I was responsible for parent education I had the pleasure of meeting many teenage parents. They are subjected to the greatest prejudices, many of them unjustifiably.

One girl I remember became pregnant at the age of sixteen and the boy who had made her pregnant was no longer on the scene. She had a good relationship with her parents and made the decision that she wanted to continue with the pregnancy. She was very mature, recognised that she'd made a mistake and now was taking responsibility for it. She'd signed up for a college course, complete with crèche facilities, and turned out to be absolutely outstanding as a mother. She breastfed the baby and continued to do so when she started college. Six months later she wrote to me and said everything was going well and she was feeling very happy and positive about life. I was absolutely delighted for her.

There was another young mum who I had some doubts about – she seemed completely unaware of what she was letting herself in for. She had the baby and was overjoyed that it was a girl. She reappeared eighteen months later, pregnant again, and was very happy about it – it seemed that in motherhood she had found her vocation. She started looking after other people's children and ended up with four children of her own. She's an amazing mum and her own children and those she looks after all adore her.

Another girl who came to the classes was a big disappointment to her own mother, who had also got pregnant as a teenager and regretted it. She too turned out to be a great role model and years later I discovered that she was going into schools giving talks to teenagers about the realities of having a baby at a young age.

Caseloading is a system of care that's on offer to more vulnerable women, including teenagers. We have integrated teams of midwives who work closely with other professionals to provide a comprehensive care package. The caseloading midwives go to GPs' surgeries and see the women there during their ante-natal appointments, then when the women come into the hospital in labour, they are looked after by a midwife from the caseloading team. Afterwards they receive post-natal care from the same team.

My colleague Julia looked after a woman who was booked in for a home birth on the battered single-decker bus where she lived with her partner and children. The family led a pretty alternative lifestyle! Needless to say, we were quite concerned about her giving birth in an environment without running water or other proper facilities, and what's more, they were never in one place for long – they kept parking their bus on various bits of land in the area, and the council kept moving them on.

Although we encouraged the woman to consider having her baby in hospital, she was determined to give birth at home ... on the bus. As midwives our statutory duty is to attend to a woman when she's in labour, wherever that might be.

The first challenge for the midwife attending the birth was to find her way to the field where the bus was currently parked. She received a call just after midnight from the woman's partner to say she had gone into labour. He gave a rough description of how to get to this field in the middle of nowhere. There was no signal for mobile phones and he had contacted the midwife from a nearby phone box.

Thankfully, somehow, the midwife managed to find her way to the bus, although there were no street lamps nearby and she had to pick her way through the long grass in the inky darkness. Once she arrived at the bus, her heart sank because there was still very little light. Midwives really do need to be able to see what they're doing! The family had a generator, but it didn't have much fuel left in it and the woman's partner was worried that it might pack up at any moment. The couple hadn't made any plans for someone to look after their two older boys, aged eight and ten, but fortunately they were fast asleep and completely unaware of all the fuss going on around them. Their mum appeared to be taking the whole thing in her stride, too, and explained that she had previously had two normal births.

The midwife could only hope that the same would be true for the third one. If anything went wrong, it would be a while before an ambulance crew could find their way to such a remote and badly lit spot.

The bus had had the seats taken out and basic kitchen equipment had been installed, along with bunk beds for the two older boys and an old mattress that the couple slept on.

'As soon as I arrived I checked her over,' Julia told me. 'She was a lovely girl and her partner made me a nice cup of tea. There was nowhere comfortable to sit, so I sat on the step of the bus even though it was a rather chilly night in November. Both the woman and her partner seemed very relaxed and the atmosphere was very nice.'

The woman was in established labour, but was not very far along. It can be very hard to predict just how quickly a woman will progress in labour when she's had one or more babies previously – sometimes things can move extremely fast, and sometimes they don't.

'As I was monitoring the baby's heartbeat, it suddenly dipped. This doesn't necessarily mean that anything's terribly wrong, as the heartbeat can slow momentarily and then pick up again, but I decided I better get a second midwife involved and asked the woman's partner to go back to the phone box to call another of the midwives on duty.'

The second midwife also managed to locate the bus and the two of them worked together to help the woman. When they needed to use the toilet they had to get off the bus and go behind a tree.

The baby's heartbeat didn't give any further cause for concern, the woman progressed slowly and steadily and ended up successfully pushing out her baby – a daughter. It was about 5 a.m. when she was born – not quite dawn at that time of the year but getting towards the end of the night.

'The atmosphere of any birth is lovely, but as we all toasted the new arrival with another cup of tea, the vibes on the bus felt particularly special. Happily the older boys remained asleep and the generator lasted out. They woke up to a lovely surprise a few hours later. The whole thing was wonderfully relaxed. Soon after the birth the bus moved on and I never saw the family again,' said the midwife.

Occasionally our statutory duty to be with a woman wherever she births can be tricky if, for example, the woman chooses to have her baby at home against medical advice. Midwifery supervisors must ensure that practice is safe. Every midwife has a supervisor to make sure we're doing what we should be doing and that we're doing it safely. If a woman is not following our recommendations, the supervisor would speak to her about why she is making those choices. If she continues to insist on doing things her way, a plan will be put in place to support the midwife and whoever attends to her at home would be supported. In these cases, where women choose to go outside of our professional recommendations, we involve our consultant midwives who meet with the woman and spend time talking her through her decision and making a plan of care. The plan is shared with the midwife supervisors and the wider team so that everyone is clear what actions are in place to support the birth.

Sometimes women have reasons for not wanting to give birth in hospital, even if they are going against medical advice. Some have a phobia of hospitals or had a poor experience first time round. Others choose to be at home for religious reasons and say that the outcome is in God's hands and that whatever happens will be God's will. Some women feel they want to give birth naturally at all costs and say they've weighed up the risks and on balance want to go ahead with a home birth. Our responsibility is to make sure the women have as much information and evidence as possible to help them make an informed choice. Sometimes the outcome has not been positive but in these cases women tend to take responsibility for it.

The caseloading midwives work very closely with families and get to build up a lovely, trusting relationship with the woman and her family. The midwives on the team all work very closely together and all support each other. One midwife, Alice, was looking after a woman who had given birth to twins on labour ward a few hours earlier. Alice was taking over from a colleague who had delivered the babies, and was looking after the mum and her twins post-natally when her phone rang. It was one of her colleagues saying that a woman who was due to have her first baby in hospital had phoned to say her waters had broken. Alice's colleague said she would go round to her house to assess whether or not she was in established labour, to save her an unnecessary trip into hospital. As it was this woman's first pregnancy, Alice assumed it would take a while before anything much happened. Her colleague assessed the woman, said she was only one centimetre dilated and that she expected it would be a while before anything happened. She left the woman and told her to call back when her contractions got stronger and closer together.

Then Alice received a call from a different colleague to say another woman who was having a planned home birth had gone into labour. This was her fourth pregnancy and she had a track record of quick births. Alice said she'd leave the hospital and join her colleague as quickly as possible, so she handed over the care of the new mum and her twins to one of the hospital midwives and headed off. It was around 3 a.m. when she arrived at the woman's house, assuming that by now the woman would be on the verge of delivering. In fact, nothing very much seemed to be happening so they all sat down and had a cup of tea and a chat.

Then Alice received a frantic phone call from the first woman in labour, who was in great distress and said she felt the baby was about to come. Judging by the noises she was making it sounded as if the baby was indeed on its way. Alice was amazed because just an hour or two before she was only one centimetre dilated.

'I'm on my way,' she said. 'But you need to call 999 as well, just in case you need to get to hospital quickly.'

Alice grabbed her drugs box and raced across to the woman's house, which was about fifteen minutes drive away. The road where the woman lived is one where the numbers don't follow any logical sequence, and some of the houses are off the main road down little side alleys. It was 4.45 a.m. and pitch black. Alice couldn't find the flat anywhere and enlisted the help of a teenage boy, who happened to be wandering around in the street.

'You've got to help me,' she said. 'I'm urgently trying to find a woman who's about to give birth.'

He disappeared down a dark alley then called out to her, 'It's down here, there's someone screaming! Good luck, nurse!' Then he wandered off. Alice raced up the stairs, found the front door open and rushed in. The woman was in the lounge screaming and panicking. Alice reassured her that everything would be okay, but then to her horror she realised that she had left all her equipment, apart from her drugs box, at the other house, such was her haste to get to the woman's side. It was clear that the woman was about to give birth and wouldn't make it to hospital. Alice called a colleague to come to the house and thankfully she and a couple of paramedics arrived just as the baby was about to be born.

When the woman's partner had phoned 999, the operator said he might have to deliver the baby himself. He was horrified at the prospect and said he couldn't do it, so of course he was incredibly relieved when the cavalry arrived! He clearly wasn't coping well with the sight of all the bodily fluids, so the two midwives sent him into the kitchen with the paramedics to have a cup of tea, leaving the woman, her mother and the two midwives in the lounge. The baby was born not long after that. 'Everything about it was fantastic,' said Alice. 'The paramedics cheered from the kitchen when they heard the baby utter its first cry. Afterwards the mother had a nice, hot bath and curled up in bed with her new baby. After a bit of a mop up of the lounge floor, nobody would have known that anything untoward had happened!'

Of course, the woman who Alice thought was going to have a quick labour turned out not to be in labour at all and didn't give birth until two weeks later ... sometimes that's just how it works out. And I'm happy to say that all the babies Alice came into contact with that night are doing very well!

One midwife I know attended a *very* strange home birth. The woman lay quietly on the bed, surrounded by a circle of people. The atmosphere was really quite creepy – nobody moved and everyone was silent throughout the labour. The room had mirrors on the walls and ceilings, so the labour was reflected all around the room, which would have been quite disconcerting if you ask me. To the mid-wife's relief, the birth was very quick and straightforward. She wasn't used to seeing herself reflected all over the place whilst she worked. Still, perhaps it's a good training exercise to see your technique from all angles!

A colleague of mine told me recently about a woman who lived in quite a remote spot on a hillside. There was a field on one side of the house and you couldn't see another soul for miles around. She went into labour on a very hot day and by the time she was fully dilated she was quite dis-tressed, but the midwife who was looking after her had the whole situation under control.

'Let's go into the garden for a few minutes, it might calm you down,' she suggested. She had a lovely garden, and getting out of the house into the fresh air seemed to help. The sky was blue, the sun was beating down and the birds were singing. The garden was filled with the fragrance of lavender.

'I want to give birth right here in the garden,' the woman said, suddenly. It was a place where she felt very com-fortable. Her husband brought out pillows, the delivery kit was set up on the patio table and sheets were laid out on the ground for her. There were runner beans on one side of her and marigolds on the other, and the midwife joked that depending on the sex of the baby, she would have to name them after one or other of the plants surrounding her. She gave birth to a beautiful, healthy baby in a wonderful, natural setting. It was such a lovely memory to have for a first birth.

Another woman gave birth in a darkened room in front of a log fire. Another, who had had two boys and longed for a girl during her third pregnancy, gave birth to a healthy girl while Christina Aguilera's 'Beautiful' was playing softly on the radio in the background. It was very fitting. When everything goes smoothly, home births really are wonderful.

12

TALES OF THE UNEXPECTED

Sometimes you just need things to make nights more attractive. I like to spoil them sometimes so I make brownies or banana cake. Naomi Colburn calls it orgasmic cake.

Ros, episode 6

ROS

When a baby decides it's ready to come out, there's not much anyone can do to stop it. The ideal situation is for the woman to be calmly prepared when she goes into labour, either at home if that's where she's planned to have the baby, or in hospital. But things don't always work out quite so conveniently . . .

The hospital car park is quite a popular venue for births, although not a particularly salubrious one. I delivered one baby in the front seat of a car at about 2 a.m. outside the front entrance of the hospital. It was a bitterly cold night, and I ran out and called to colleagues to bring blankets and equipment. We managed to get her trousers off and saw that the baby's head was already out – there wasn't too much for me to do, to be honest. Needless to say, the front seat of the car was a bit of a mess afterwards!

One woman gave birth in the back seat of a car in the hospital car park watched over by two very large and very ferocious Alsatian dogs. The midwife who was looking after her kept trying to persuade the woman to get *out of* the car, but she refused. The midwife was too scared to get *into* the car with the dogs and felt she had no choice but to leave the woman birthing in the car with a couple of dogs overseeing the proceedings instead of a trained professional.

For some reason these car park births always tend to happen in the middle of freezing cold winter nights, but as soon as I get the call, all thoughts of how chilly it is out there vanish. The adrenaline kicks in and whooshes through my veins. I grab a wheelchair, a towel and a blanket and race downstairs in the hope of reaching the woman before she actually gives birth. We always try and get the woman and baby inside the hospital where it's warm and clean before delivering the placenta. Everyone tends to be on a real high after these births, as long as mum and baby are doing well. We really do feel the sheer, unstoppable force of nature on these occasions.

Sometimes though, women who have planned to give

birth in hospital don't even get as far as leaving the house because the whole thing happens so quickly. In those cases we have to talk the woman's partner through the whole process over the phone.

'Let the baby's head come through. Is the baby okay? Keep the cord attached and try not to deliver the placenta. Is the baby crying and pink and does it have good resistance in its arms and legs?' We hope that the answer to those questions will be yes, and then a midwife can finish off the job of delivering the placenta and cutting and clamping the cord.

While some births are quick, others are positively supersonic. One midwife was chatting away to a woman who was having very mild contractions and didn't appear to be in any discomfort at all. Suddenly she scrunched up her face, gave an almighty push and out popped her baby's head. Her proper labour had lasted for no more than a minute!

Almost as popular a birth venue as the hospital car park, and even less desirable, are toilets. It's not as rare as you would think for babies to be born in toilets. Sitting on the toilet opens up the pelvis, making it easier for a baby to be born. And while it might seem strange to think about popping to the loo when you're about to give birth, some women are less aware of their contractions than others so may not know that their baby is literally about to put in its first appearance while they relieve themselves. Babies generally don't come to any harm when they arrive in the world this way, as long as they're scooped up pretty quickly. I remember looking after one woman who was having only mild contractions. She went to the toilet and as she sat down the baby was suddenly born! Fortunately the baby wasn't face down in the toilet and I managed to swiftly retrieve it and all was well.

We tend to find that the 'unexpected' births are more common amongst teenagers than older women. Often they don't want to admit to themselves or their families that they're pregnant. One night I was called to A&E, across the road from the Princess Anne. A teenage girl was there with her parents – she was clearly in labour, but apparently had had no idea until now that she was pregnant. I delivered the baby for her and wondered whether she might have known all along, but chosen to keep the truth from her parents. She delivered the baby, which was on the small side but okay. We wrapped her up and brought the new mum and her baby over to the Princess Anne.

Years ago we had something called the 'flying squad', which went out to women in labour who weren't going to make it to the hospital in time. A doctor and a midwife would grab a box of equipment and race to the woman's address. This service has been disbanded now because it was decided that an ambulance could reach the woman more quickly. In the flying squad days, I was called out to a teenage girl who was giving birth three months before the baby was due. When we arrived at her house, the girl was lying on the floor and had already given birth. She was certainly a lot more than six months pregnant and she and the baby seemed fine. We cut the cord and delivered the placenta and I started chatting to her.

'Did you know you were pregnant?' I asked.

'Yes,' she replied, sheepishly.

'Did your mum know?'

'No.'

'You took a big risk concealing this pregnancy and not accessing ante-natal care,' I said to her. 'There are some conditions that are sometimes more common in girls of your age, and they could have put you and your baby at risk. If you get pregnant again, you must go to your GP so that you can get proper care.'

She confessed to me that she had actually sat an exam that day, even though her contractions had started. Her mum wasn't at home, but I offered to call her to break the news to her that she had just become a grandmother. I was surprised to find that her mother didn't sound as shocked as I would have expected.

'I *knew* she was pregnant,' she said. 'I asked her several times and she insisted that she wasn't and had just put on a bit of weight, but I knew in my heart that she was.'

Being a midwife can sometimes lead to unexpected surprises. A friend of mine was standing in a queue in a shop one day and was being kicked hard by a toddler in a buggy who was behind her in the queue. The child's mother was distracted and hadn't noticed what she was doing. The midwife raised a very stern eyebrow at the toddler, which made her stop kicking immediately. Then the mother noticed the midwife and exclaimed, 'Oh, hello! Fancy seeing you here. You probably don't recognise my little girl now, but you delivered her!'

The midwife felt very embarrassed and tried her best to smile politely and enquire about the toddler's development. We may recognise the mums if we see them again after they've given birth, but we certainly don't recognise the babies once they start growing up!

It's not only the midwives who have embarrassing moments. One new mum raised the alarm when she found blood in her bed and was convinced she was having a post-partum haemorrhage. We treated the case as an emergency, but after taking a thorough history and examination, no blood or apparent problems were detected. We were all baffled about the cause of this sudden bleeding, which appeared to have stopped as mysteriously as it had started.

Suddenly the woman clapped her hand over her mouth. She looked thoroughly mortified and admitted, 'I've just realised what the problem is. I was absolutely ravenous after I gave birth last night and was eating toast and jam in bed. Some of the jam must have spilt on the sheet and stained it ...'

After our panic had subsided and we realised she wasn't

about to bleed to death, we discharged her and had a good giggle about the whole thing. I'm sure that's the last time she ate snacks in bed!

MARIA

Midwives who work in the community sometimes have to deal with some very unusual situations. When a midwife gets a call from one of the women she's been looking after saying that she's gone into labour, she jumps into her car and races to the woman's home as fast as she can. It's fair to say that she's so focused on getting to the woman in the shortest possible time, she doesn't always notice what's going on around her.

One of my colleagues had rushed over to the home of a woman in labour who lived in Southampton's red light area. She was concentrating so hard on the task in hand that she didn't notice a prostitute standing in the doorway of the block of flats she was about to enter. As she walked towards the flats, wearing her midwife's uniform, a man rushed up to her, and said, 'How much d'you charge, darlin'?'

The midwife looked at him blankly for a minute before the penny dropped. He thought she was a prostitute dressed up as a nurse!

'Don't be ridiculous!' she said, briskly. 'I'm a midwife and there's a woman in this block of flats who will be giving birth alone if you don't step aside so I can get into her flat.'

The man looked on open-mouthed as she raced up the stairs, no doubt more than a little bit disappointed!

Late one night, one of the community midwives, Barbara Gormley, received a phone call from the husband of a woman in labour. The woman's midwife was not on call and Barbara said that she would get to the woman as quickly as she could. The caseloading midwives always cover each other's cases.

'Hurry, hurry! I think she's going to give birth very soon!' her husband said. The midwife promised to get there as fast as she could, but said she didn't know exactly where they lived, as she hadn't been there before. The husband said he'd go and stand at the end of the road in his anorak and wait for her there, so he could guide her to the flat. He sounded very anxious on the phone and once again asked the midwife to be as quick as she could.

The midwife jumped into her car and drove as fast as she could to the woman's home. It was about 3 a.m. when she arrived at the road where she had agreed to meet the husband. Sure enough, there was a man in an anorak. She screeched to a halt, flung open the passenger door and shouted to the man,

'Quick, get in! Just get in!'

Looking a little shell-shocked, the man got into the car.

'Right, so which way now? I need to get to your wife before she gives birth, do I need to turn left or right?'

The man looked at her, blankly.

'What? I haven't got a wife who's about to give birth,' he spluttered.

Barbara looked at him in horror.

'What do you mean? Wait … are you not …? Why *on earth* did you get into the car?'

'I'm on my way to do an early shift … you pulled up looking all panicked and told me to get into the car. I thought there was some sort of emergency so I just got in!'

Barbara apologised profusely to the man, before she shooed him out of the car and sped off to find the man she was really looking for. Eventually she managed to find him, standing at the end of the street, wondering what on earth had happened to her. They just managed to get to the woman before she gave birth to a lovely, healthy baby.

All midwives are keen to deliver the hospital's first baby of the new year. Just before midnight one year, a porter alerted us to a woman screaming in pain in a car outside the main entrance to the hospital. We ran down the corridor gathering gloves, instruments and towels on our way. But by the time we got to the hospital entrance the screaming had stopped. We'd brought a wheelchair and asked the woman to sit in it.

'No, no I don't need it, I'm all right now,' she smiled.

The baby had been born into the leg of her trousers, still surrounded by the membrane. We burst the protective fluid sac and the baby gave a healthy cry. He was absolutely beautiful. That night none of us won the race to deliver the first baby of the new year – he had delivered himself!

13

THE MARCH OF TECHNOLOGY

You beat the forceps! What can I say? You goddess!

Dominique, episode 3

ROS

Birth is now much more hi-tech, and sometimes having too many machines in the room can make the woman lose touch with her natural instincts. It's important to preserve women's natural instincts during the process of birth, and to interfere as little as possible with that. Women need to be given an expectation that they can give birth naturally, even though it's reassuring to know that the technology is in the background if it's needed. Of course it's important not to idealise birth too much – it *is* painful and things *can* go wrong, but at the same time it is a normal human process that women's bodies and minds are cleverly designed for.

When I was a student we always used pinnards – a kind of ear trumpet – to listen to the baby's heartbeat during a woman's pregnancy and labour. In some ways, midwives have been deskilled because we don't use them as regularly now and we rely on machines to give us information. But we have had cases where the machine has recorded a heartbeat, supposedly the baby's, and it turned out later that the machine mistakenly recorded the woman's heartbeat and the baby was sadly dead.

With a pinnard you can't make that sort of mistake, because you *only* hear the baby's heartbeat. But modern life is ruled by machines and people feel dependent on and reassured by them. We have machines for taking blood pressure and for recording pretty much every medical observation you can think of. It would be very sad if we lost the skill of palpating a woman's abdomen and estimating the size of her baby. Having said that, although we have lots more machines to monitor than we ever used to have, the basic process of labour and birth has remained unchanged for centuries. In terms of the technology and the mechanism of having a baby – the instruments like the little cord scissors and the instrument to clamp the cord – much remains the same; there are some things you feel will never change. But of course, there are always new theories coming out. When we were training, you delivered a baby in gloves and a gown and there were bottles of warm Savlon that we kept in a cabinet. Then ideas changed, and the idea was that babies should be born in a clean, not a sterile environment and some people moved away from washing the woman at all. There's also been a big debate about whether the midwife should have their hands on or off the baby's head – there are lots of different ideas around. I'm a hands on the head midwife, it's just personal preference.

Ante-natal scans are a major development from how pregnancy was managed in the past, and they are amazing. This advance in technology means that babies with problems are born in the appropriate place with the best possible medical back-up. Before ultrasound scans, we sometimes thought a woman was having one baby but then two appeared – we rarely get that kind of a surprise any more. The twenty-week scan is very accurate, and can pick up problems with a baby's heart, lungs, bones, head and kidneys. Nevertheless, we do sometimes get unexpected Down's Syndrome births. Some women who are in high-risk categories for Down's opt for amniocentesis and choose to continue the pregnancy if the baby tests positive. However, there are also some cases involving low-risk women who have not been tested and give birth to a Down's Syndrome baby. Down's Syndrome is a condition that's there for life and changes everyone's plans. When a baby is born unexpectedly with Down's Syndrome, we try to be as supportive as possible to the parents and also to give them as much information as we can about the condition. There are many fantastic support organisations that can provide help for families in these situations, and we always suggest that they get in touch and make the most of the help that's available.

One amazing medical advance is fetal blood sampling. This involves taking a blood sample from the baby's head, which is then run through the machine and can tell us whether or not the baby is coping well in labour. To be able to do this the cervix needs to be at least four centimetres dilated. We would only take a sample if we had concerns about the baby – for example if the heart rate was dropping. If a woman is less than four centimetres dilated and changing her position and giving her fluid doesn't make any difference to the baby's heart rate, then she would be rushed down to theatre for an emergency Caesarean. If the baby's heartbeat is the only indication that it might be in trouble, the doctors have to make a judgment call about whether or not to perform an emergency Caesarean, and it is one of the hardest decisions they have to make. No one wants to subject a woman to unnecessary surgery, but at the same time no one wants to risk the baby being damaged by not getting it out quickly if there's a problem or potential problem. It's very hard for the doctors and sometimes they're fishing in the dark.

Babies in the breech position are more likely to be delivered by Caesarean these days. At thirty-seven to thirty-eight weeks, the doctors try to rotate the baby externally, but if it doesn't work the woman is offered an elective Caesarean. Sometimes if a woman is having twins and the first baby is in the right position for a straightforward delivery, they are more willing to deliver a second twin who's in the breech position.

In the UK our Caesarean section rate runs at about twenty-one per cent. In the US it's much higher than that, as it is at some hospitals in Australia. We do sometimes get women screaming for a C-section because they don't want to experience labour or because they had a bad experience with a vaginal birth first time round. If they request a Caesarean during their second pregnancy because of a bad experience previously, we refer them to our consultant's clinic and they can have a proper talk about what went wrong last time. If the woman has had a long labour and a traumatic forceps delivery she will understandably be dreading the prospect of going through all that again. But we can reassure her by explaining that she will dilate much more quickly the second time and the pushing stage will also be much quicker. Sometimes the traumatic memories are still very fresh, but if a woman has had a previous vaginal delivery the doctors are very reluctant to do an elective Caesarean, although they'll consider it if there was a rectal tear last time. There's often a lot of negotiation around that. For women who had a Caesarean last time, we encourage them to try a vaginal birth second time round, depending on the reason why they needed a Caesarean for their previous birth.

When women or their partners or family members beg us to perform a Caesarean and we refuse because there's no clinical indication that they need one they often think we're being very unreasonable and cruel.

We hear stories of celebrities who have elective Caesareans followed by a tummy tuck while they're still lying on the operating table. They emerge days after child-birth, ready to show off their washboard stomachs with a photoshoot. Well, that certainly doesn't happen on the NHS. The surgeons get the baby out, stitch the woman up and then off she goes.

Drugs have also advanced – there are new drugs to control blood pressure and others to stop premature labour. If a woman's blood type is rhesus negative and her blood is destroying the baby's blood, they can do a transfusion through the cord while the baby is in the womb.

Some of the biggest advances are in neo-natal care. The equipment we use now is quite mind-blowing. Twenty years ago a baby at twenty-four or twenty-five weeks would die, but now many more are surviving. The boundaries are getting pushed back further and further. Now they are able to save twenty-five-week babies weighing just 500 grammes. Parents of twenty-three- and twenty-four-week-old babies expect them to survive.

There is a limit, though, to the size of baby they can actually save. These babies spend a long time in the neo-natal unit and when they finally do go home may be reliant on oxygen for some time. They have collapsed lungs, brain haemorrhages, and may end up with gut infections, necrotic bowels which rot, so that they need colostomies. There are huge ethical questions over when it's right and when it's wrong to prolong the lives of these tiny babies. We can use the best that technology has to offer but we may be condemning a child to a lifetime of medical care and a very poor quality of life. Does the family have the resources to cope with all that? It's all very difficult and I wouldn't want to be the person making that decision. Technology opens up a huge moral and ethical can of worms. People expect you to be able to do miracles like on the television dramas, but sadly it isn't always as simple as that.

We get fewer multiple births as a result of IVF treatment than we used to, thanks to technological advances. When fertility treatment was in its infancy and the drug Clomid was used, there were a lot more multiple pregnancies and a lot of the babies didn't survive. These days no more than two embryos are implanted. We get quite a few IVF twins and quite a lot of spontaneous twins as well. With twins the ideal is to give the woman an epidural and manage the labour in theatre so that everyone is on standby in case of any problems. The birth of the first twin is usually more straightforward, but there may be a delay between the birth of the first and second twins and the second one is more likely to be lying in an awkward position.

One of the biggest technological changes we've experienced is the increasing use of the internet by women and their families to research anything and everything connected to labour and childbirth. I'm all for women being better informed about pregnancy and childbirth but the axiom 'a little knowledge is a dangerous thing' also applies here. Women sometimes read up about all the terrible things that can happen in pregnancy and childbirth then convince themselves that they're afflicted with various life-threatening conditions, when in fact they're fit and well and are having a perfectly normal pregnancy and birth.

Although there have been so many advances in this field of medicine, we still need to expect the unexpected. Just as there are sometimes babies born in poor condition with no prior indication that there's any problem, machinery can sometimes indicate a problem and yet the baby will emerge pink and healthy. We know an awful lot about labour and childbirth, and technology has an important role to play. However, when human beings are involved it's impossible to have total certainty about anything.

MARIA

Although there have been huge advances in areas like neo-natal care, to a great extent birth is birth and hasn't changed that much over the centuries. We do have a greater tendency to rely on technology to support our assumptions about how a pregnancy is progressing than we used to and I don't think that's necessarily a good thing. A midwife uses her eyes, ears and hands to interpret the signs and symptoms of an impending birth. The use of these senses and of a midwife's knowledge and intuition are invaluable assets and should never be underestimated or sidelined by technology. I believe that technology should only ever be used alongside our own experience and skills, rather than as a substitute for them.

We are trying to reduce the Caesarean rate. I think birth has moved too far towards intervention and now we're trying to pull it back. The reality is that Caesareans carry many more risks than a vaginal delivery – it's fine to use Caesareans if the risks of a vaginal birth outweigh the risks of a Caesarean in a particular case, but it's not a good idea otherwise.

Women in this country are fortunate enough to have maternity services that are rigorously monitored for high quality and safety standards. They not only have access to high-calibre midwifes, but also to first-rate obstetric care if either mum or baby require additional help or intervention. But we must remember that technology is there to support us and the work we do, and not the other way round!

Midwives have a responsibility to maintain safe practice and all have a named Supervisor, who will be an experienced practising midwife who has undertaken additional education and training to support, guide and supervise her colleagues. They are there to develop and maintain safe practice to ensure the protection of mothers and babies.

14

BRINGING UP BABY

Do you think it's time to make a gentle move?
That's fine, let me make a call to the unit – make
sure they've got the red carpet out, the
champagne on ice, the complimentary flowers.
The way it's been this week, you've had to book
early to avoid disappointment.

Dominique, episode 3

MARIA

We do encourage skin-to-skin contact between a newborn baby and its mother when it's appropriate. It's a lovely thing for a mother to have her newborn baby placed directly on her skin, and it can really help them to bond. If a baby is left to its own devices, it will root around to find a source of food, but it won't necessarily want to do that within seconds of being born and sometimes we can be a bit too quick to put the baby to the breast. Rather than shoving the nipple in the baby's mouth, we try to let the baby find its own way.

We're trying to rewind things a bit and revert to more natural and instinctive practices both during and after birth – allowing a new mum and baby to take their time and enjoy the profound moment of skin-to-skin contact. We are trying to declutter birth – usually birth will just happen naturally and we should be there as a bystander to support that. It saddens me that we're now talking about 'normalising' birth as a significant change. It shows how far we've strayed.

Breastfeeding is a practice we actively encourage, while accepting that not every mother will make that choice. Some women can be put off breastfeeding by peer-group pressure; others see their breasts as a sexual thing, rather than a source of food for their baby. On the other hand, there are women who feel under enormous pressure to breastfeed and that's something we also have to be aware of. Readmission of babies with feeding issues is predominantly a problem for those who are bottle-fed, and we advise all mothers to breastfeed unless a baby specifically needs to be prescribed bottle milk. We are trying to improve breast-feeding rates, because it's accepted that unless the mum is HIV+, breastfeeding is the best option. But we don't want women to end up feeling like failures, and if a woman chooses to bottle-feed our role is to support that.

While breastfeeding is a wonderful, natural thing to do and enhances bonding between a mum and her baby, it would be helpful if women had a bit more information about some of the tricky realities. The books don't tell you that you need towels in your bed when you're sleeping to prevent your milk from leaking all over the sheets and leaving a horrible smell when it dries.

It was a complete shock to me when I discovered that one breast leaked while I was feeding from the other one. When my children were babies, I had a little Mini and one time I was driving with my daughter in the car and she was desperate for a feed. I pulled over, jumped into the passenger seat and fed her there. I ended up squirting milk all over my Mini – including under the dashboard! I didn't discover quite how extensively my milk had sprayed around the car until I came to sell it years later and I gave it a thorough clean.

A friend of mine also had an embarrassing experience with her car whilst breastfeeding. She had broken down round the corner from her house soon after she gave birth. She called out the AA man and when he arrived she was so relieved to see him that she ran towards him. Unfortunately, the running stimulated her breasts and milk began pouring from them. She folded her arms tightly across her tee-shirt while she tried to explain to him what had happened to her car, hoping and praying that he wouldn't notice her soaked top.

Generally mums should eat whatever they want when breastfeeding, but some babies do react to strawberries, and they're not too fond of strong curries. It's also best to avoid peanuts.

I remember one woman who chose to get pregnant at the age of thirty-five. She opted to get impregnated by a friend because she didn't have a partner. After the baby was born she just dropped everything, stocked up on ready meals and devoted herself to breastfeeding the baby on demand. If women are able to go with the flow it can make the first few weeks of life with their new baby so much more enjoyable.

ROS

The practice of putting the naked baby against the mother's skin immediately after birth is currently in vogue. Skin-to-skin contact is good for the baby because it gets the baby used to the smell of its mother's skin and the rhythm of her heartbeat. It can be a lovely thing to do and we would encourage it if that is what a woman wants. But not everyone wants their baby smeared with various bodily fluids and prefers for them to be washed and wrapped in a blanket before being handed over for the first cuddle. Some women are so exhausted by their labour that they literally don't have the strength to hold their baby and ask for it to be handed to their partner.

Some babies will want to feed straight away, but the baby might also be exhausted and not interested in an immediate feed. In some circumstances getting the baby to latch onto the nipple is impractical in any case. If the woman has had a Caesarean, for example, she can't very well start breastfeeding on the operating table, and if she's losing a lot of blood there will be more urgent priorities. An early breast-feed is a good idea if it works for the mother and the baby, but flexibility and practicality is key.

We definitely recommend and promote breastfeeding and there's lots of information about it available to women during pregnancy. If a woman is undecided we say, 'Why don't you try it? You might find that you enjoy it and it's the best thing for your baby.'

Being a new mother can be a very insecure time. A lot of mums do get hung up on what other mums' babies are doing and worry that their baby isn't doing as well as others. For women who are feeling a bit low, it can be damaging to their self-esteem to hear about other perfect babies and their apparently perfect ability to feed from the breast. Better maternity leave arrangements are making a huge difference though. It means that mothers have more time to spend with their babies, are more relaxed when it comes to feeding and caring for them and can see their babies doing things for the first time, instead of leaving it to the nanny or the childminder to witness the precious first smile or step.

On the post-natal ward we give a lot of support to

women trying to breastfeed and follow-up when they go home. There are a few women with very flat or inverted nipples which can be hard for the baby to get hold of and suck – we used to use nipple shields but they aren't very fashionable these days. Smaller babies may get tired when sucking and can't do it as well as the bigger ones. The milk comes in on the third day after the birth and at that point women often feel quite weepy. Their breasts are very full and it's good to know that even when they've been discharged from hospital they can call on us. We want breastfeeding rates to be as high as possible. They'd probably be higher if we had more staff resources to visit women at home the first ten days after birth to offer them support with breastfeeding and help to iron out any problems they're experiencing.

I remember one woman who gave birth to a baby girl a few weeks early. She really wanted to breastfeed but it was hard to get the baby to latch on because it was so small. She started off by expressing breast milk and we squirted it into the baby's mouth through a syringe. Then we squirted breast milk from the syringe onto the nipple so the baby got the taste for milk on the nipple. After that the baby started to feed directly from the nipple. It's very rewarding to help establish successful breastfeeding when there has been a bit of a problem at the beginning.

Babies are very attuned to their mothers' emotions, so if the mother is very upset the reflex which makes the milk flow won't work so well. If her bottom is too sore to sit on it might be better to get her to lie on her side to feed. If she has a sore Caesarean scar it may be better to tuck the baby under her arm like a rugby ball to feed it. With twins a mum sometimes starts off feeding them separately but if she can feed them in tandem she will save herself a lot of time. Mums breastfeeding twins have to make sure they're not too hard on themselves – feeding two babies is very tiring and time consuming. What matters is making sure that the mum is resting and eating and drinking. As long as she eats, the baby eats and she gets some sleep, that's all that matters. Mums of twins become experts at eating while they're feeding without dropping the food on the baby's head! Some mums do one feed breastfeeding one and bottle feeding the other then change the babies round for the next feed. There are no breastfeeding police who are going to come round and fine you and tell you off for that. It really is a case of finding what works best for the individual mother.

If breastfeeding doesn't work for a mum because she finds it awkward or embarrassing or she struggles to get her baby latched on, she shouldn't feel bad about trying an alternative method of feeding. Lots of women read baby books avidly and feel like failures if they're not doing what the books say they should be doing, but women need to be a bit kinder to themselves. The main thing is that both mother and baby are happy and healthy.

When it comes to bathing and nappy-changing it can be

quite frustrating to stand by watching new mums because they take such a long time getting to grips with this whole new world. That first meconium nappy goes absolutely everywhere and it takes quite a bit of scrubbing to get the baby clean. We encourage the mums to be as relaxed as possible about things like bathing their babies. As long as their faces and bottoms are clean – as well as folds of skin under their chins where vomit and dribble can settle and cause infection – mums shouldn't worry too much about constantly cleaning the other bits.

Some dads think the baby will break when they first hold it. We try to reassure them and tell them to make sure the baby's head is well supported in the bath. We explain that they won't hurt the baby as long as they don't bend a limb in a way it isn't meant to go. While of course it's important to keep the baby safe, they don't break that easily and can cope well with firm but sensible handling.

Although there are many different ways to be a good mother, I do think that some mums are 'naturals' and others are not. A lot of it is down to the personality of the woman. Some women are better able to go with the flow than others, and if they're relaxed, the baby is more relaxed. Some worry about everything and read every book under the sun, but too much worrying can take away the enjoyment of having a baby.

We're always on the lookout for signs of severe post-natal depression. With this condition mothers have lost touch with reality. We try to get them into specialist units where they're watched all the time and are prevented from harming themselves or their baby.

Often the women who are prone to post-natal depression are the ones who are less able to adapt their previous lifestyle to accommodate the demands of a new baby. They are used to being in control of all aspects of their life and suddenly they're faced with this tiny human who makes its own decisions about when it's going to sleep, eat and cry. The women who are happy to go with the flow – allowing the house to descend into chaos for a while and leaving the shirts un-ironed without worrying about it – are less likely to suffer from post-natal depression during this period of significant adjustment.

The best way to get through the early weeks and months with a new baby is to try to filter out as many of the deadlines and demands of normal life as possible, to suspend the usual priorities and instead surrender to the (non) timetable of the baby.

EPILOGUE

To share this moment in a couple's life – that's one of the best things about being a midwife. Becoming a mother is one of the most amazing jobs in the world, and I don't think you can beat that.

Lorraine, episode 4

MARIA

As midwives we seem to occupy a special place in people's consciousness. I remember a gentleman stopping by my house one evening, unexpectedly. Our paths had crossed in the past and he knew I was a midwife. He came to ask if I could give him some professional advice because he thought his daughter was miscarrying. His wife was sitting in the car outside and, of course, she was very upset about the whole thing. He had come all the way to my house simply to ask me what his daughter should do. He asked me if I would speak with his wife in the car and offer her some words of comfort because he didn't know what to do. I sat with her and suggested that her daughter should see her GP. 'All you can do is be there for your daughter,' I said. 'It may be that she'll get over this episode of bleeding and the pregnancy will continue, but she is very early in her pregnancy and miscarriages are not uncommon at this stage.'

This incident made me realise just how much being a midwife is part of your whole life – not just a job that you leave behind when you leave the hospital. I was very humbled by the fact that this man, who I didn't know well, had come to see me that evening. There wasn't anything I could do for him, his wife or his daughter, really, but if people know you're a midwife they will come to you and talk to you about things they wouldn't normally talk to other people about. They see us as someone who can help out in a crisis. Sometimes just being there, listening and caring can make a huge difference to people when they are experiencing pain and trauma.

A positive birth experience is one where the mum feels satisfied with the care she has received and embarks confidently into her role as a mother. And there are many different ways to achieve that outcome. Birth is a very raw experience and encapsulates so many different feelings:

pain and anguish and joy and exhaustion – it's not called labour for nothing. They say that one of the reasons why labour is so tough is to prepare mothers for the demanding job ahead of being a parent.

Labour is a unique experience – it's all about doing the right thing for the person at the right time. It's about flexible care, making sure that the only outcome you're focused on is the best outcome for that particular mother and that particular baby. It's a marvellous thing to be part of. I've had some lovely thank-you cards from women following their baby's birth, and it's nice to know you've made a difference and helped to make childbirth a really positive experience for them. I often receive feedback from mums telling me about the fantastic work midwives have done. We midwives are just people who are passionate about our work, love the women we work with and go home happy when we know we've helped to make a woman's birth experience a safe and happy one.

The magic of helping a child to be born never fades, no matter how many years you work as a midwife. It's something that's hard to describe and it certainly isn't something you can capture in a bottle. I feel incredibly privileged to be doing this work and wouldn't want to do any other job. Midwifery really takes your heart and soul. So much of our lives are so ordered and controlled and as a result we can lose touch with our instinctive, primal side. But the pain and process of labour takes women back to that state. The sophistication of our society thankfully hasn't eroded that link between a woman and her newborn baby. When things go well, there is no joy in life quite like that which accompanies the birth of a child. Midwives share that joy, helping a woman go through the exacting experience of labour to their prize of a beautiful baby at the end of it. Many midwives stay on at the end of their shifts from time to time so that they can remain with a woman in labour until she's given birth. We develop a lovely, special relationship based on trust. There's nothing we love more than waving off new parents with their precious bundle when they leave the hospital after birth.

Midwifery is the kind of career that you're either cut out for or you're not. Some of the students on my midwifery course went off and did other things after their training, because they realised that the job wasn't for them. The midwives I work with absolutely love their jobs, and for them and for me it really is a calling. For anyone who loves the idea of supporting a woman through the challenges of childbirth and helping to bring a new life into the world, this is the job for you. But it certainly isn't nine-to-five and it can be very emotionally draining – as a midwife we're there for the highs and the lows of birth.

The moment that a baby is born is a pure and miraculous one. Just as we all have unique DNA, every birth is unique too. To be part of that special moment for a woman when she finally gets to meet the brand new life that she has spent nine months carefully growing inside her and to hold a brand new baby before any of the world has been imprinted on it is quite simply the best job in the world.

ROS

The urge to procreate is so powerful that sometimes it can quite literally take your breath away. Even women who had a bad birth experience first time round, and swear they'll never have a baby again, have such a strong drive to reproduce that many do get pregnant again. They say that there's something in nature that makes women forget much of the suffering of childbirth, so that they go on to have more babies, however painful or difficult the first birth might have been.

The relationship that a woman has with her midwife has a huge bearing on how she feels about her labour and birth. It is a unique partnership. The midwife and the woman work together as a team to bring about the best possible outcome and it is a privilege to be able to support women during this major life event.

Trust is a vital part of our relationship with women. I

know that if I lied to a woman, she'd just stop listening to me. If a woman asks me a question and I don't know the answer, I admit it. If a midwife says something that a woman doesn't want to hear, she's the easiest target for the woman's anger.

Most women are fantastic in labour and behave with incredible dignity. Some women who've had miscarriage after miscarriage and are in labour with their first live baby show amazing strength of character. I really do admire their determination to keep trying to have a child.

We're constantly striving to make birth the most positive experience possible. That's much more likely to happen if women go into the whole thing with a flexible attitude – being prepared to expect the unexpected and not having too rigid a birth plan. Labour can start low risk but things can change quickly and suddenly, especially with a first baby.

Some women feel they're being weak or have failed if they have an epidural. But the reality is that for some, gas and air won't be enough. Women need to be realistic. A really good relationship between the woman and her birth partners helps as well. The atmosphere in the room goes a long way towards making birth a positive experience. When I go into a room and everyone is smiling and chatty it makes a huge difference to how the woman feels. When there's a friendly attitude in the delivery room, you feel as if you've been welcomed into the woman's family, albeit temporarily, and it does make the job much nicer. Humour also goes a long way to easing the tensions and stresses of labour. We try our best to keep the channels of communication flowing so that the woman and her partner are not in the dark about the various developments in the course of labour.

If I've looked after a woman right through my shift and I know that she's likely to give birth quite soon after my shift finishes I might stay around to see things through. All midwives are at liberty to do this but they need to be aware of their own limitations and decide when they have ceased to be safe. If the woman is in the middle of pushing I'm usually keen to stay – after all the hard work of getting through labour for both the woman and the midwife there is an enormous sense of satisfaction in seeing that baby born. And needless to say, we midwives do love delivering babies!

I've worked nights for fourteen years and the hours can be a bit more anti-social than a day shift, although thankfully my family have been very tolerant. I joke that they'll end up in therapy in their mid-thirties because of my absences, but so far the children seem fairly well adjusted!

I've always loved working nights though. The day-to-day administration of the hospital is over and the entire focus is on the women giving birth rather than on bureaucratic or political matters. And one of the best things about working nights comes at about 6 a.m., just as the sun is rising – we make the biggest plate of hot buttered toast and have a cup of tea and a chat. It means the night shift is nearly over, keeps us going until the morning, and let me tell you, it's the best tasting toast ever.

Sometimes this work can be very hard. It's physically tiring being on your feet all the time and it's emotionally and psychologically draining too. But we're incredibly privileged to be sharing in this hugely exciting moment in the lives of new mothers. We do our best to let women know that they matter to us and that we appreciate how special this time is for them.

You never know what kind of case is going to come through the door. A woman can start off low risk but suddenly her condition can become very complicated. You constantly have to think on your feet, multi-task and prioritise. Labour can be progressing spontaneously and then suddenly the baby can be in distress – you have to be constantly aware that these things can happen. The important thing is to recognise this kind of change immediately and respond swiftly.

Sometimes it's hard for women to understand that there are no right and wrong ways to give birth. All that matters is that there's a happy and positive outcome with a healthy mother and a healthy baby walking out of the hospital. I was very disappointed with my own first birth. I'm blessed – or cursed, depending on which way you want to look at it – with a very good memory and could remember every detail of my first labour. It took me a long time to get over it, which spoilt the first few weeks with my new baby. I felt I was cheated out of those special early weeks with her because I was still recovering from the birth.

I planned the second birth differently and stayed at home for longer before going to hospital. When I got there and discovered I was still only four centimetres dilated, I was so disappointed and felt I'd done it all wrong again. But this time the pethidine and gas and air worked very well for me. Although the pushing was hard, I got over the second birth much more quickly and that helped to lay my unhappiness about the first birth to rest. And then I went on to have my third and fourth babies at home.

I firmly believe that every experience you go through you learn from and often you can learn more from the bad experiences than the good ones. My own experiences have helped me to give encouragement and advice to other women. Of course midwives who haven't had their own children are just as good at offering sound advice, but sometimes they have to work hard to convince the woman that they're still there for her and that they know what they're doing.

Being a midwife is hugely rewarding, there's no other

job like it in the world. At the end of a shift I might not have delivered any babies but I hope I've made a difference to that woman and her family. I try to take time to explain things, to reassure, to give advice about how to cope and to give good care. It's nice to feel that by being there you have made a difference. It's a real privilege when you earn the trust of women you've never met before. Mums-to-be put a lot of trust into their midwife and we have to be sure we don't let them down.

What we should learn as midwives is that we have the power to make the childbirth experience better than it otherwise would be. Our mothers and grandmothers had a real understanding and intuition about women's bodies and it's important that we continue to protect and preserve that instinctive knowledge alongside the stuff we learn in the textbooks.

Being a midwife is something that follows you around. Although we don't remember every woman we've looked after, they usually remember us. It's always funny when we bump into people in their post-pregnant, everyday lives. It's sometimes hard to recognise a dressed, flat-stomached woman when you've only seen her near naked and with a bump. A friend of mine was at the hairdresser's having her hair done one day. She was chatting away to the hairdresser and in the course of the conversation said that she was a midwife.

'I knew it!' the hairdresser exclaimed. 'I was sure it was

you who looked after me when I gave birth. I had a baby at fifteen and he's now nineteen. I remember there was a mirror in the labour room and you said to me, "Look at your mascara, it's all ruined. The sooner you push this baby out the sooner you can reapply your mascara!" In the middle of all my agony in labour, I laughed.'

Her son is twenty-four now and every so often she brings him in to see that midwife. It's lovely when mums keep in touch and we have an opportunity to see the baby we delivered growing up.

I think that midwifery is a calling. Not everyone is cut out to be a midwife and although it certainly isn't an easy option, I can honestly say that I've loved every minute of my career as a midwife. There's never a dull moment and every woman, every baby and every birth are unique so I never get to feel that my work is repetitive in any way. There are many times when I'm completely physically and emotionally exhausted and when I have a good cry when there's been a sad outcome to a birth. But even when there is bad news, it's a privilege to be able to offer support to women and their families. Childbirth in the UK in 2011 is an incredibly safe process and in the vast majority of cases the outcomes are happy. I can't think of anything more wonderful than helping to bring a new life into the world – in fact a lot of my job is one, long celebration. Birth is such a miracle. I can truly say there's nothing in the world that I'd rather be doing than this.

WHATEVER HAPPENED TO ...?

For the families who take part in One Born Every Minute, *getting used to the idea of being filmed during labour is only the beginning of an exciting journey ... once the cameras stop rolling, they have a brand-new, helpless baby to take home and, whether it's their first baby or their third, many adjustments to make to their lives. Read on to find out what happened to some of the most memorable couples who took part in the first two series.*

SERIES ONE

Lisa, Will and Jack, episode 3

Lisa and Will's baby Jack had a condition called Gastroschis, which means his stomach had an opening through which his bowel had protruded, and he required special care after he was born.

Jack's condition was detected in the twelve-week scan, and a plan was put in place to care for him in the neo-natal unit immediately after his birth.

Lisa had a Caesarean under epidural, with Will by her side, and baby Jack was taken immediately to the neo-natal unit. After an operation to correct his condition and eight days in intensive care, Jack was able to go home when he was one month old. Lisa says that he has been a wonderfully placid, easy and healthy baby from the moment they brought him home.

'I've only had three sleep-deprived nights in a whole year,' she says. 'He's started walking now and has turned into a real little person. I went back to work after nine months but I really enjoy all the time I spend with him when I'm not working. My philosophy is that the washing can wait until tomorrow!'

Lisa is pregnant with her second baby, which is due in April 2011, and she's hoping that the next baby will be as easy as Jack has been. As a result of featuring in the first series of *One Born Every Minute*, Lisa has been recognised a lot in the street and has had overwhelming support, especially on Facebook.

'One woman came up to me in the supermarket one time, told me how touching she had found our story and gave me some money to put in Jack's money box for him. It was such a lovely thing to do.'

Joy, Fabio and Ellie, episode 4

Joy and Fabio are delighted with their daughter Ellie, although both admit to finding the experience of looking after a baby much more physically exhausting than they had expected.

Joy was closely monitored during her pregnancy and labour because of her diabetes. The baby was conceived through IVF treatment and Joy's labour had to be induced.

It took several days after the process was started for Ellie to be born. Fabio camped out in Joy's room in an armchair with a blanket over him during the long wait. Baby Ellie was finally born by Caesarean and was welcomed into the world by her ecstatic parents.

'Having a baby is everything we ever dreamed it would be,' says Joy. 'It doesn't really matter that we're tired all the time. Having her is worth every minute of the exhaustion we experience. Ellie has started talking and we love watching every moment of her development. The best thing of all is when she comes up to us and gives us a big hug.'

Joy says that they often get recognised in the street by people who saw them in the first series of *One Born Every Minute* and have been contacted by old friends they had lost touch with who saw them on TV.

'People often come up to us and say hello. They're really lovely. I'm so happy that we appeared in the documentary. We had been trying for a baby for so long and having the birth recorded on TV gives us a lovely, special memory to look back on.'

Sheilagh, Richard and Fraser, episode 6

Sheilagh was rushed to theatre for an emergency Caesarean section and needed a general anaesthetic, which meant that

Richard could not be with her in theatre. This can be a very hard time for the partner and staff tried to support Richard as much as possible. Sheilagh said she had no particular expectations about how the birth would go and she was delighted and relieved that baby Fraser was born fit and well after the drama of the birth.

Because she had a general anaesthetic the cameras weren't allowed into the operating theatres. 'At least I got away without having the birth filmed!' she joked. 'My midwife, Michelle Comrie, was absolutely fantastic. Having her looking after me made all the difference.'

She says that Fraser has been a very easy baby and a complete delight from the word go. 'He just sits in his pram while I look after the horses on the farm,' she says. 'He's a very cool baby and fits in with everything we do. Being filmed was a positive experience for us. I do get recognised a lot in the street and in the supermarket and people are always lovely and supportive.'

Penny, Ben and Isla, episode 6

Penny had very clear ideas about how she wanted her labour and birth to be and wanted Ben to help her fulfil them. Everyone was impressed with their open and honest relationship, as well as their understanding of the challenges labour might present and the roles they were about to play as parents.

Penny and Ben have enjoyed every minute with their baby Isla. 'She seems so happy all the time,' says Ben. 'She sleeps through the night, we think she's trying to say "dada" and she's crawling ten to the dozen. She can stand up and has taken a few faltering steps.' He added that Isla has taken over their lives much more than they anticipated she would, both physically and emotionally.

'We've just sort of evolved to fit in with her needs,' said Ben. 'We do still manage to do some of the things we did before though, like going out to a pub or restaurant. We take her with us and she sleeps through the whole evening!'

Charlie, Dan and Izzy, episode 7

Charlie gave birth to twins prematurely at twenty-three weeks. Sadly one of the twins died and Izzy, the surviving twin, had to spend several months in hospital and after she was discharged was dependent on oxygen for several more months. The good news is that Izzy now at home, and happy and healthy, and no longer needs the oxygen.

'We've got a daughter called Jodie who's seventeen months older than Izzy, and she never had any health problems. She saw a health visitor twice and we got her weighed now and again and that was all. It's completely different with Izzy. Paediatric nurses come to the house once a week to check on her progress, and the doctors and hospital are still a big part of our lives. The hospital will always have a special place in our hearts, because without them Izzy wouldn't be here. We owe the amazing medical team everything.

'I had reservations about being filmed but in the end it helped going through that process. I hope that seeing what we went through and how well Izzy is doing now will help others, too. We got so much support from people, getting in touch with us via the internet, saying that they had also had babies born at twenty-three weeks who were doing well. We get recognised in the street, too and people are so lovely when they come up to us.'

Izzy has made lots of progress and can roll over and sit up. 'Her lungs are weaker than other babies', which makes her more susceptible to infections, but generally she's doing fantastically well,' says Charlie. 'She's amazing. She couldn't be more of a miracle.'

SERIES TWO

Tendayi, Maxwell and baby Maxwell, episode 2

Tendayi had an epidural when she was in labour, when the pain got too much for her to bear. It brought her some relief and she and her partner Maxwell were thrilled with the arrival of Maxwell junior.

Going from life before baby to life after baby has been a huge adjustment for the couple but they're enjoying every minute of their time with him.

'Every day with Maxwell is special in its own kind of way. He's at the stage now where he's starting to talk. Sometimes he tries to imitate us and it's so funny to hear him do this,' she says. 'We're from Zimbabwe and we speak our mother tongue, Shona, to Maxwell at home but he speaks English at nursery. He's already bilingual.'

Tendayi received a leaflet about the *One Born Every*

Minute series while she was attending ante-natal classes and she and Maxwell decided to get involved.

'We thought it would be a nice memory for our baby to have when he's grown. I don't think the presence of the TV cameras made us do things any differently,' says Tendayi, 'except that we spoke to each other in English, not Shona.'

Tendayi's family in Zimbabwe were surprised that she had agreed to give birth on television.

'When I told my sister I'd done this crazy thing she couldn't believe it. Something like this would be a complete no-no in Zimbabwe. I'm very excited about returning there and showing the baby off to all our friends and family. I keep promising to send them a DVD of the episode we appeared in but I haven't got round to doing it yet.'

Since having Maxwell, Tendayi has embarked on a nursing degree.

'It's very hard fitting my studies around childcare but I'm keen to advance myself. I was working as a carer before and I would really love to become a nurse. Maxwell helps to look after the baby but we're always very tired. Life has changed so much. We can't be as spontaneous as we were before Maxwell came along. Pre-baby I could make an arrangement with a friend at the last minute. Now I can't say "see you in five minutes" because I have to organise Maxwell's food and nappies before we leave the house. Everything takes much longer to organise.

'I'm so happy that we got involved with the series. Everyone was great and there was no negative side to it at all. I know that lots of people watch it because children are part of almost everyone's lives.'

Donna, Wayne and Emelia, episode 3

Donna agreed to be considered for inclusion in *One Born Every Minute* but never for a minute thought she'd be chosen. She was attracted by the promise of broadcast-quality footage of the birth, even if her story wasn't selected for the series.

'I was convinced that I wouldn't be going through the whole experience of giving birth in front of millions of viewers,' says Donna. 'It seemed like such a great opportunity to have a major event in our lives professionally recorded that I decided to go ahead. It was a bit of a shock when I found out that I was actually going to be on TV after all!

'My sister was with me during my labour, as well as my husband Wayne, and she's promised me that if she has a baby I can be there for her birth,' she adds.

Emelia is Donna and Wayne's second child and Donna says she adapted much more quickly to the new arrival this time around.

'She's a lovely little girl with a real mischievous twinkle in her eye. She's definitely got me under her thumb, she's a real mummy's girl,' she laughs. For Donna one of the best things about being filmed was being able to watch the first few hours of Emelia's life over and over again. 'Those changes that happen to babies during the first few hours of life aren't something that could be captured in a single photo or even a series of photos. I'd go through the whole process of giving birth on TV all over again just to have those first precious hours on record.'

Donna was convinced that she would swear continually throughout her labour and was mightily relieved (and slightly disbelieving) when she watched the footage that there wasn't a single swear word in evidence.

She thought that perhaps a few people might recognise her and Wayne for a couple of days after the episode they featured in was aired. But fifteen months on she's still being stopped in the street.

'Everyone is lovely and positive about seeing us on the programme. Nobody has said anything negative at all.'

Donna works for a fostering service. She witnesses many difficult situations where children are separated from their birth parents for a whole variety of reasons and says that doing this work has really made her count her blessings.

'Working for a foster care service makes me really appreciate being a mum and having my own children with me all the time,' she says. 'It's just such a wonderful thing.'

Lucy, James and Benjamin, episode 4

Lucy had expected that giving birth for the third time would be a breeze. She had had a difficult labour with her first baby but had sailed through the second one and assumed that the third would be as straightforward. But the baby was breech.

'His head was under my ribcage and his legs were dangling down,' recalls Lucy. Two consultants tried and failed to turn him and later it became clear why. Doctors discovered that the cord was wrapped three times around the baby's neck. Lucy had a Caesarean and thankfully everything was fine.

Lucy and James both say that baby Benjamin is an absolute joy.

'We call him our surfer baby because he has blonde hair, bright blue eyes and tanned skin!'

Lucy and James took part in *One Born Every Minute* because they had decided that Benjamin would be their last child and they thought it would be nice to have a lasting record of the birth.

'Lots of people recognised us from the series and some women said that watching me deal with Benjamin being in the breech position had given them confidence to deal with problems that might arise in their pregnancies.'

Lucy and James say that their family is definitely complete now.

'Benjamin is the most good-natured baby you could ever wish to meet. We feel very lucky and blessed to have all our children and to have such a happy family,' says Lucy.

Hayley, John and Tyler, episode 7

Although Hayley's labour and birth was filmed by a cameraman, unlike most of the other births which were captured by fixed cameras in the delivery room, both of them felt very relaxed about the whole thing.

'People told us when they watched Hayley give birth on TV that we came across as "very natural",' says John. Things progressed very quickly during the later stages of Hayley's labour but, as John puts it, when she was eight centimetres dilated 'the baby didn't want to move'. Hayley needed to have an episiotomy and forceps and the delivery was quite tense, but happily everything was fine in the end.

John says that appearing on TV has been a huge boost for Hayley's confidence.

'People were sending messages to Hayley on Facebook and stopping her in the street to tell her how well she'd done. We have had a lot of people recognising us. They think they've met us somewhere before but can't quite remember where!'

The couple are loving every minute with baby Tyler,

although their sleep quotient plummeted when six of his teeth came through at the same time.

Meeting Hayley was a turning point in John's life and becoming dad to Tyler was a crowning moment in the couple's happiness together.

'Just before I met Hayley I had split up with my ex and didn't have full custody of our daughters. Just before we went on *One Born Every Minute* I gained full custody of the girls so it really made our family complete. Going on TV was a perfect happy ending for us.'

John says that the knowledge that the cameras were rolling during Hayley's labour made him feel 'less useless'. He set his mind on being as helpful and useful as he could possibly be to Hayley and he too received many lovely and supportive comments from viewers. And the interest in the family doesn't appear to have waned.

'People are really interested in the progress Tyler is making and they still ask us to see pictures of him as he grows,' says John.

Carol, Kevin and Martin, episode 10

Carol was keen to take part in the programme, not just so that she could share the special and unique experience of giving birth with the nation at large, but also to give hope to other women who suffer from the same conditions as her. She had endometriosis and was overweight at the time that she conceived. Doctors warned her that she would have difficulty conceiving and that her weight could be a barrier to a healthy and successful pregnancy

'Despite what the doctors said I actually conceived very easily and although I got a lot of stick from the doctors, I had a great pregnancy. I didn't experience any problems at all,' says Carol.

Carol had previously experienced great sadness, losing her first baby on the night of her mother's funeral, perhaps because of the great stress and sadness she was going through. She was overjoyed when she conceived again very soon afterwards. Despite the words of dire warning issued to her by medical professionals during her pregnancy, she said that when she went into labour everyone was incredibly kind and supportive.

'The staff at the hospital were absolutely wonderful. I just couldn't fault them at all.

'Martin is fourteen months old now and he's absolutely great. He's always cheerful and he giggles a lot. Our lives are a hundred per cent better since he arrived. He really is the light of our lives.'

Martin has become a very active toddler. He started walking at ten months and is now a keen climber. He's not saying many words yet but makes himself understood with his own unique system of pointing and grunting.

'Martin has made me look at life differently,' says Carol. 'Before I was worried about my career but now I'm much more focused on my family. Having Martin has been such a positive experience for me. I hope that going on TV has helped send a message to other women who have similar health issues to me that they can have good pregnancies and give birth to healthy children.'

A QUICK HISTORY OF MIDWIFERY

For as long as there have been babies, there have been midwives. Perhaps they had no official title, or recognised role, but one way or another, women have always helped each other in labour. Someone is needed to comfort and support a woman who is giving birth and to deliver the baby. Traditionally, it has been women, rather than men, who have taken on that role.

The first written references to midwives appear in the old testament (*Genesis 24*), although the word 'midwife' was not used until much later. It is derived from the Middle English word *mid* meaning 'with' and the Old English word *wif*, meaning 'woman'.

Midwifery was a recognised female occupation in ancient Egypt, but they jealously guarded the secrets of their profession, so unfortunately very little was handed down in writing. In the second century, the physician Soranus of Ephesus described the ideal midwife as

. . . literate, with her wits about her, possessed of a good memory, loving work, respectable and generally not unduly handicapped as regards her senses [i.e., sight, smell, hearing], sound of limb, robust, and, according to some people, endowed with long slim fingers and short nails at her fingertips.

Pliny, another physician from this period, valued nobility and a quiet and inconspicuous disposition in a midwife. Midwifery seemed to be a respectable and valued profession in which women could earn a living; they had a similar status and income as male doctors.

The midwife's main role was to assist in the birthing process, although they may also have helped with other medical problems relating to women. Midwives and physicians both believed that a normal delivery was made easier when a woman sat upright, so midwives used a stool with a crescent-shaped hole through which the baby would be delivered. The birth stool or chair often had armrests for the mother to grasp during the delivery, and a back which she could press against.

The midwife sat facing the mother, encouraging and supporting her through the birth. When the baby was delivered, it was wrapped in a piece of cloth, the umbilical cord was cut, and then it was washed and sprinkled with 'fine and powdery salt to soak up the birth residue, rinsed, and then powdered and rinsed again'. After the delivery, the midwife made a decision about whether or not an infant was healthy and fit to rear. She inspected the newborn for congenital deformities and tested its cry to check whether it was robust enough to survive.

In medieval times, childbirth was considered so deadly that the Christian church told pregnant women to prepare their shrouds and confess their sins in case of death. Midwives played an important role in emergency baptisms and as such were highly valued by the church. A popular medieval saying was, 'the better the witch; the better the midwife'; to guard against witchcraft, the church required midwives to be licensed by a bishop and swear an oath not to use magic when assisting women through labour. Childbirth was regarded as a 'disease of women'.

One of the first schools for midwives was established in the early sixteenth century at the Hotel-Dieu, in Paris. The first woman to write a text on midwifery was Louise Bourgeois (1563–1636), the wife of an army surgeon. Midwifery was seen as a respectable profession and generally women in this field earned a good living, depending on the social class of their clientele. A midwife had a vested interest in the delivery of healthy babies since she received an additional fee from the godparents at the time of baptism. There was no equivalent school in England since girls were not trained in Latin, the language of medicine. There is recorded evidence of midwives sometimes being overzealous and pulling the baby out too vigorously, ripping off one or more of its limbs in the process or causing damage to the mother. If a baby's limb got stuck, a midwife might chop it off to speed up the birth. Thankfully things have changed since then!

Midwives were licensed by the church because they often had to baptise dying infants. The midwife's oath included helping poor women as well as rich ones, not allowing a woman to falsely name a man as the father of the child, not to use cutting or dismembering and to register the birth with the church and the authorities.

William Smellie (1698–1763) is believed to have had a major influence on the development of midwifery. He became a midwifery instructor and wrote several influential texts on the subject of pregnancy and childbirth. Before the end of the eighteenth century there were six or seven maternity hospitals as well as maternity wards attached to General hospitals. However, during the eighteenth century, a division between surgeons and midwives developed, as medical men began to assert that their modern scientific processes were better for mothers and infants than the folk traditions of many midwives. By the beginning of the nine-teenth century, wealthier women had their babies delivered by surgeons. Augustus Granville, founder of the Obstetrical Society of London, thought that women were 'unsuited by nature for all scientific mechanical employ-ment'. But midwives persisted in their campaign for midwifery to be recognised as a profession and in 1881 the Midwives Institute was founded and began arguing for increased and better training. It later became the Royal College of Midwives. In 1902 the Midwives Act became law and midwifery became an established profession in Britain. Midwives now had to undergo supervised training and registration.

At the turn of the century there was very little ante-natal care for pregnant women. A woman was rarely examined until labour was under way, although she was given information about general health and diet during pregnancy.

In 1946 the National Health Service Act opened a new chapter in the history of public health. It promised a comprehensive medical service for the whole population including the provision of midwives and health visitors.

GLOSSARY

Abruption When some or all of the placenta detaches from the wall of the uterus before the birth of the baby.

Breech When the baby's bottom is the presenting part.

Cord prolapse When the cord descends in front of the baby's head.

Epidural Pain relief administered by an anaesthetist into the spine.

Episiostomy An incision made into the opening of the vagina.

Folic acid A vitamin supplement taken before and during the pregnancy to help the development of a healthy baby.

Fontanel Soft spots on the baby's head where the skull bones meet.

Forceps Two metal instruments shaped to fit around the baby's head to aid delivery.

Gas and air A mixture of Nitrousoxide and oxygen gases for inhalation, to support pain relief.

Incubator A piece of equipment where a baby can have a temperature-controlled environment, used for premature or poorly babies.

Meconium The first bowel movement passed by a baby.

National Childbirth Trust A charitable organisation concerned with education for pregnancy, birth and parenthood.

Neo-natal unit A specialist unit for premature or sick babies immediately following birth.

Pethidine A pain relief administered by injection during labour.

Placenta The organ that develops and attaches to the wall of the uterus. It transports oxygen and nutrients to the baby via the umbilical cord.

Pre-eclampsia A condition that is peculiar to pregnancy. Symptoms include high blood pressure, swelling and protein the urine.

Resuscitaire A portable piece of equipment providing heat, oxygen and suction if required after birth.

Shoulder dystocia When the shoulders of the baby become

lodged above the pubic bone after the delivery of the head.

Skin-to-skin contact When the baby is placed naked on the mother's bare chest.

Sure Start A government initiative targeting children under school age in deprived areas, promoting health, play and community involvement.

Ventouse When a suction cup is applied to the baby's head to aid delivery.

Vitamin K A vitamin that is given by injection to the baby following birth to aid the blood–clotting mechanism.

USEFUL INFORMATION

What to do if you think you're pregnant:

- Take a home pregnancy test: ask your pharmacist about which ones are the most reliable
- Make an appointment with your GP. If you don't have a GP, find your local one at: *www.nhsdirect.nhs.uk*
- Abortion services and counselling from BROOK counselling: *www.brook.org.uk*

Pregnancy health:

- General Health Information: *www.healthtalkonline.org*
- Diabetes in pregnancy: *www.diabetes.org.uk*
- Information about maternity services and choices for maternal health: *www.nhs.uk/Planners/pregnancycareplanner/Pages/Conceptionhome.aspx*
- Antenatal results and choices, helping parents and professionals during antenatal testing and its consequences: *www. arc-uk.org; www.fetalanomaly.screening.nhs.uk*

Advice and support for new parents:

- Children's health: *www.nhs.uk/**start4life***
- NCT: *www.**nctpregnancyandbabycare**.com*
- *Birth to Five:* Published by the Department of Health, available from their website: *www.**dh**.gov.uk/publications*
- Mumsnet: *www.**mumsnet**.com*
- Advice for breastfeeding: *www.**nationalbreastfeeding helpline**.org.uk*

How to become a midwife:
- Royal College of Midwives: *www.**rcm**.org.uk*
- Association for Improvement to Maternity Services: *www.**aims**.org.uk*

Information on the series:

- *www.**lifebegins**.channel4.com*

ACKNOWLEDGEMENTS

One Born Every Minute was an adventure we embarked on wanting to provide an honest and open insight into the unique moments experienced at birth by women and families that we are privileged to be part of.

We would like to thank everyone who has been involved in the journey from the television series to the writing of this book.

Our respective husbands and children who have enthusiastically encouraged us throughout:
Mike, Rebecca and Jacob
Simon, Erica, Duncan, Matthew and Megan.

The families involved in the series.

Colleagues and staff at the Princess Anne Hospital.

The production team at Dragonfly Film and Television.

The midwives whose birth stories helped to shape the book:

Eileen Brosnan
Julia Clark
Lorna Bird
Tina Parker
Sonia Bannatyne
Alice Dale
Jacqueline Hayes
Florinda Fernandes
Barbara Gormley
Michelle Comrie
Lisa Falls

Diane Taylor for her ability to listen and scribe our stories

Alison Ayres and Sarah Cole from the SUHT communications team, whose support has been invaluable.

Southampton University Hospitals NHS Trust for allowing us the opportunity.

. . . and finally but without whom our job would not exist, the amazing women whose stories we have shared.

Maria Dore and Ros Bradbury